ICETE Series

Is It Working? Researching Context to Improve Curriculum

ICETE

Global Hub for Evangelical Theological Education

Langham

GLOBAL LIBRARY

Is It Working? Researching Context to Improve Curriculum

A Resource Book for Theological Schools

General Editor

Stuart Brooking

ICETE

Global Hub for Evangelical Theological Education

Langham

GLOBAL LIBRARY

Published 2018 by Langham Global Library
An imprint of Langham Publishing
www.langhampublishing.org

Langham Publishing and its imprints are a ministry of Langham Partnership

Langham Partnership
PO Box 296, Carlisle, Cumbria CA3 9WZ, UK
www.langham.org

ISBNs:
978-1-78368-333-8 Print
978-1-78368-442-7 ePub
978-1-78368-444-1 PDF

This publication was made possible through the generous funding of Overseas Council Australia.

British Library Cataloguing-in-Publication Data
A catalogue record for this book is available from the British Library

ISBN: 978-1-78368-333-8

Cover & Book Design: projectluz.com

The fast-changing world we are living in is facing unprecedented challenges: economic, technological, social and personal. Meeting these challenges calls for new educational priorities or even new paradigms of education. This book helps us to rethink how to develop our curriculum in view of our socio-cultural context and challenges us to establish educational priorities in fulfilling the mission of the church. The generous sharing of these theological education institutions and various leaders involved in curriculum revision has opened our eyes to see the importance of sensitivity, openness, innovation, and collaborative efforts in bringing the needed changes. This book is definitely an invaluable resource book for institutions determined to have impact in this age.

Rev Luke Cheung, PhD
Professor in Biblical Studies,
Vice-President, China Graduate School of Theology, Hong Kong

Is It Working? extends the reach of the stimulating presentations and discussions on impact assessment at the ICETE 2015 Consultation in Antalya. It provides theological institutions with a helpful framework for assessing the effectiveness of their training programs and in implementing a "research-driven curriculum revision" to strengthen their impact on the church and in society. Several examples from the field were presented to flesh out the concept. These serve as an inspiration for theological schools to take on the challenge of investigating the impact of their graduates and making the necessary curriculum change informed by research data. Furthermore, this book calls accrediting agencies to focus more on the assessment of outcomes and impact in their accreditation of programs. This invaluable resource is a must for all leaders and educators serious about maximizing the impact of their training programs!

Theresa Roco-Lua, EdD
General Secretary, Asia Theological Association

What a great initiative to make this book available – an ideal tool and resource based on the last theological educators forum (ICETE 2015). The continuous development of methods and approaches will bring tremendous benefits for the global church through theology studies.

Márcio Matta
President,
Associação Evangélica de Educação Teológica na América Latina (AETAL)

This book argues that theological education benefits when we dare to ask the question: Is what we are doing working? As the leader of SAIACS and one of the participants in the research-based curriculum review process that led up to the ICETE 2015 conference, I agree whole-heartedly. The testimonies show each institution learned unique and valuable things.

I began with some qualms – Should *usefulness* be the criterion of impact? Are we humans *responsible* for kingdom outcomes? Does action trump contemplation? To echo Marven Oxenham's fine article, does "Martha" trump "Mary"? I decided that such research-based review needn't fall into these traps, and it sure beats keeping our eyes shut! In fact, in SAIACS' case, we discovered employers and alumni both wanted more "Mary" emphasis on spiritual formation.

This book will encourage more theological education institutions toward confidence they are meeting their goals. It certainly helped SAIACS towards "excellence for the sake of mission."

Ian W. Payne, PhD
Former Principal,
South Asia Institute of Advanced Christian Studies (SAIACS),
Bangalore, India

Contents

Acknowledgments

Thanks to the generous donor who has made this volume possible, including the English, French and Spanish editions. He understood the importance of the whole project for the mission of the church.

Thanks to Jo Bailey who also assisted. Jo skilfully proofread the articles, and in some cases assisted by taking the lecture notes of busy presenters and turning them into suitable written pieces. Not only that, but as a lover of God and his mission, she said she loved reading the articles and was encouraged by the contributors' honest grappling with complex issues and their desire to glorify God in all ways.

Thanks to Dr Perry Shaw who generated the questions at the end of each chapter, and gave encouragement for the project along the way.

Thanks to Marion Brooking, my wife, and to the Lebanese media company One-16, who took the photographs from the ICETE 2015 conference. These feature throughout the book.

Thanks to Dr Riad Kassis of ICETE, and the Langham Literature leadership, under whose imprimatur this book goes forth.

This book is dedicated to the people of God who long for leaders who are well taught in the sacred Scriptures, so they can affirm and challenge their cultures, and thus lead the church to fulfil its mission to worship the Triune God in all the world.

Rev Dr Stuart Brooking
Editor

Preface

Engaged and Effective!

Since 1980 the International Council for Evangelical Theological Education (ICETE) consultations have been the principal international forum for professional reflection and interaction among evangelical theological educators worldwide.

"Rooted in the Word, Engaged in the World" was the theme of the ICETE 2012 international consultation in Nairobi, Kenya. Two questions arose from this theme. Though rooted and engaged, how do we know that we are effective in what we do? Is it possible to measure the impact of theological education on church and society? To respond critically to these two fundamental questions ICETE held its international triennial consultation in Antalya, Turkey, from 6 to 11 November 2015.

The uniqueness of the Antalya consultation was seen in three main areas. First, the consultation from its earliest conception was an expression of serious collaborative efforts for almost three years between Overseas Council Australia and USA, and ICETE. Second, the consultation was not just an event. It was a climax phase of the hard work of eleven theological schools that have been engaged in a project assessing theological education (also known as the Research-Driven Curriculum Revision) for almost two years. The consultation provided a platform for these schools to share and interact with other schools. Third, ICETE was committed to working alongside Overseas Council Australia and USA and other similar bodies to disseminate wisdom, knowledge and tools to help other theological institutions. The book that you are holding in your hands aims to fulfil this goal. Special thanks go to Dr Stuart Brooking,

Executive Director of Overseas Council Australia, for working tirelessly on editing this book, and to Langham Literature for publishing it.

It is my earnest prayer and hope that this book will contribute to the achievement of two goals. First, that theological educators and leaders will have the necessary tools to focus on the outcomes as being demonstrated in their graduates, in their ministries and in the health of the churches and organizations they serve. Second, that theological educators and leaders will be able to share the assessment tools with other institutions, and, by doing so, will connect, network and collaborate for the kingdom.

Finally, I conclude with this quote from Dr David Baer, who at the end of the Antalya consultation shared a summary that the listening groups had heard: "Yesterday morning, I found myself tapping into my notes my own quasi-Logic Chain:

> Humility . . . honesty . . . clarity . . . (repeat)
>
> Humility . . . honesty . . . clarity . . . (repeat)."

As we apply the concepts and principles outlined in this significant resource, let us seek God's Spirit so we can do that in humility, honesty and clarity.

Rev Riad Kassis, PhD
International Director, International Council for Evangelical
Theological Education

Introduction

"We Want to Know if It Is Working"

For me, this book started in October 2011. I was driving Elie Haddad, President of Arab Baptist Theological Seminary, from one speaking engagement to another as part of Overseas Council Australia's promotion of ABTS in Australia. In a casual conversation about the college and its aspirations to improve, Eli asked me this question: "Stuart, I wonder if OCA would be interested in this project that we think would be really important – though it's not an easy one to fund."

He went on to explain: "We want to know if what we are doing matters. Is our curriculum really the right one for the Middle East? We want to investigate our graduates, not just to get good stories of successes, but to test if what we are teaching them is what they need to know for what they should be doing. Are we actually making the impact we should?"

The implications of those questions are enormous. What college would be happy to discover that it is wasting its time? That it is having no real impact? Which leader would have the courage to say it out loud if that was what was found?

As those implications dawned on me, I responded, "That is very brave of you." (This favourite phrase from the British TV series *Yes, Prime Minister* was clearly in the background to the comment, and formed the topic of the next couple of minutes' conversation.) And then another problem loomed as I thought about it further:

"How would you test impact?" There are so many pious objections that will limit even the question being asked: God grows the seeds of the gospel secretly. Humans cannot see his work. It would be presumptuous to measure such a thing. Surely the success stories are sufficient.

"We have a staff member, Rupen Das, who has decades of experience in measuring impact of projects all round the world. He has done it for World Vision and many other development agencies. What we want to do is adapt the work he does, and make it to suit a seminary."

And so it was that the concept of "research-driven curriculum revision" entered the global evangelical lexicon, not for the first time, of course, but in such a way that it would take root within a few years in the whole theological scene of the Majority World.

OCA was indeed interested in the project and a donor was found who backed it over the next two years. The work they did culminated in a review panel examining not only the value of what ABTS had achieved, but also the transferability of the method to other seminaries around the world.

Phase 1 of the project was complete and Phase 2 began soon after. A sub-committee invited a small group of seminaries to apply to be part of the next process. Ten were chosen, and a conference was held in Lebanon in February 2014. Overseas Council USA Regional Directors and other consultants were engaged to continue the work through that year and the next. What ABTS had taken several years to work through, these ten were being asked to complete in eighteen months. Thankfully a number were already underway with some of the concepts for curriculum review, but for most the research of context was an extra dimension.

With the encouragement of Dr Riad Kassis and the ICETE leadership, the goal was that these eleven seminaries might present at the ICETE Triennial in Antalya, Turkey, in November 2015. The theme of the conference was "Research-Driven Curriculum Revision" and most of the material in this book flows directly out of the presentations in Antalya.

Since that time OC USA has continued to encourage an ever-widening circle of seminaries to understand the concept and implement research and curriculum change based on that research.

My hope is that this resource book will provide stimulation to many more theological institutions around the world to understand their context and change their curriculum. The ubiquitous Western-based curriculum has served the church well in some contexts, but poorly in most. This hegemony needs to be broken, so that the purity of the church is established one worldview at a time, and so that the mission of the church is truly suited to each context.

May the stories in this book inspire courage – not to copy outcomes, but to set out on a unique journey for your own theological institution.

May the questions at the end of each chapter direct thoughtfulness, challenge and critique, so you can formulate your own way of changing your curriculum. In this way the purity and mission of the church can be promoted.

Stuart Brooking, PhD
Executive Director, Overseas Council Australia

Section I

Assessment of Context

Why? What? How?

Throughout this resource book there are numerous practical suggestions, experiments, and reports of research and attempts to change the curricula of theological schools. Before all those practical "tips" are considered, it is important to set the parameters of what assessment is, from the Bible itself, and then to consider what this concept is all about. This first section seeks to put in place the scope of the project, biblically and theoretically.

In Section 2, four specific examples are given which were presented at the ICETE 2015 Triennial Conference, from Latin America, Asia and Africa.

The final section seeks to address a number of issues in leading change. The whole concept is further critiqued in the last three chapters, so that due consideration is given to the process. This book does not seek to provide a single straight-line suggestion about how things should be done. Rather, it encourages each theological school to work diligently to invent the right process for the context.

As always, we were greatly assisted at the ICETE 2015 Triennial Conference by the biblical exposition given by Dr Chris Wright. Who would have known that the first assessment of the Christian mission was linked to the very city in which we held our conference – Antalya, Turkey. As he expounded the scriptural view of our topic he led us to understand both the value and the limitations of our endeavour. The passages in both Old and New Testaments show a variety of approaches and thus both encourage and warn us at the very start.

Bricks, books, bucks and bodies are the "four Bs" of how assessment has been done historically. There is a growing awareness that more is needed to properly assess the work of a theological school. Dr Scott Cunningham leads us through the concept of the "logic model" and sets the scene for understanding the key concepts of outcome and impact. This allows assessment to go beyond the mere inputs and activities of a theological school and ask "Is it making a difference?"

The work of Rupen Das at Arab Baptist Theological School was foundational in beginning this whole project, and in chapter 3 he expands on some of the details that Dr Cunningham explains.

Dr Ashish Chrispal, as the OC Regional Director for Asia, worked with a number of the theological schools engaged in this process. In chapter 4, he guides us to see the value of well-framed assessment and how that can benefit the whole theological institution.

1

Effectiveness and Impact in Theological Education from a Biblical Perspective

Christopher Wright
International Ministries Director, Langham Partnership, UK

"Commit to the Lord Whatever You Do and He Will Establish Your Plans." Amen! But Is That Enough?

The wisdom of the wise in this verse in Proverbs is, as usual, delightfully simple and straightforward: "Plan, pray, get on with it, and God will do the rest." So long as you put in the effort and pray about it, God will make sure the results are "established."

That's how we'd like to think it will all work out when we invest huge amounts of planning, prayer, time and resources (material and human) in the grand project of theological education (TE). And there is a measure of truth in that assumption. After all, the verse makes several assumptions which apply as much to TE as to any other part of our life and work as Christians.

The verse assumes:

- that all our work and planning should be done for God and committed to God;
- that God is intensely interested (in every sense of that word) in what we do (or claim to do) for him;

- that God cares about outcomes, the *results* of our planning and actions, and wishes to see them "established."

But, as always in life, good assumptions and prayerful practice do not always produce the consequences we hoped for. So are we right to worry about consequences, and to try to find ways to measure whether or not we are being effective? Or are such concerns "unbiblical," or "unspiritual"?

I am aware that people may have come to this conference with *two possible reactions* to its title and the agenda that lies before us in the coming days.

On the one hand, there will be some who *enthusiastically* embrace the whole concept of measuring our effectiveness and impact in TE. At last, they may think, we can urge one another not merely to "do TE," but to find out whether what we are doing (and have been doing for generations) is making any tangible difference in the real church in the real world. They will be hoping for some guidance and tools for that task. And they look forward to the eventual emergence of survey results, statistics and percentages, graphs and trends, and hard verifiable evidence of what TE is (or is not) accomplishing for the greater cause of God's mission through God's church in God's world. They will welcome such information and insight for its own sake, of course, but they will not be unaware that it all makes for more successful fund-raising proposals and annual reports . . .

On the other hand, there will be some who come to this agenda with a measure of *suspicion* and reluctance. They may think that what they regard as an obsession with measurement, quantifiable results, statistics, and so on, stems from the rise of the social sciences in the modern era in the West, and operates from a worldview (that only what can be counted counts, and everything has to be empirically verifiable) at odds with Christian faith in the sovereignty and providence of God. We should faithfully get on with doing what we know God calls us to do and not be distracted into measuring results. That is God's business, and only the future will show us what he has accomplished.

I hope this brief opening presentation may say something by way of challenge *and* reassurance to both viewpoints, as we reflect on what light the Bible may shed on our endeavour.

I want to offer four areas for reflection.

- First, the Bible tells us that outcomes do matter. We do well to consider what results our actions or intentions will produce.

- Second, TE is a highly "consequential" activity. There are certainly *intended* consequences. We should ask if what we are intending aligns well or not with what the Bible has to say about the purposes of teaching within the people of God.
- Third, we can think about whether the Bible supports *planning* for effectiveness and impact, and if so, what *should* we be planning if we are to be effective?
- And, finally, we will consider the more ambiguous question about whether we can *prove* effectiveness and impact (or whether we should even try to do so).

1. Outcomes Matter (According to the Bible)

The Bible says a lot about "ends" – the results and consequences of actions, whether promised, threatened or simply recorded.

- To Adam and Eve: "Do not eat of the tree of the knowledge of good and evil; IF you do – death."
- God's constant "IF" to Israel, the context of his intentions for them, for instance, Exodus 19:4–6: "IF you will obey me fully and keep my covenant, then . . ."
- The future depends on present choices. Deuteronomy sets the choice before Israel in stark terms. Chapters 28–30, "Now choose . . ." Blessing or curse, life or death.
- The whole narrative of Old Testament Israel's history could be framed in terms of the outcomes of choices – some good (Abraham, Moses, etc.), and many bad.
- And the whole ministry of the prophets could be framed as encouraging Israel to make right choices, in order to avoid the otherwise inevitable bad consequences of bad choices being made at the time (i.e. warnings and predictions about future outcomes, intended to effect change in the present, in order to achieve different outcomes).

But what is at stake in whether or not Israel makes the "good choice"?

Answer: The mission of God for the sake of the nations.

God is looking to long-term, creation-wide, global outcomes for his great project of redemption and blessing. He calls his people to participate in that goal-oriented project. So a lot hangs on whether or not they act within that story and for the sake of its outcomes.

So our life as God's people in general (rightly conceived as our participation in God's mission) and our engagement in theological education in particular (rightly conceived as an intrinsic and intentional part of our participation in God's mission) should have an "outcomes" orientation, since all that we do is connected to the great purposeful narrative of Scripture.

The outcomes of what we do, in TE or anything else, will be either helping or hindering, either contributing to or subverting, the missional purpose of our existence as God's people.

So, yes, outcomes do matter and we ought to give attention to them.

Having said that, we need to notice that the Bible gives examples of being concerned about outcomes for the *wrong* reasons or motives.

Fear of supposed outcomes can lead to disobedience (e.g. the Israelites at Kadesh Barnea; Jonah; the parable of the talents). Or it can lead to apathy and paralysis (Eccl 11:4).

Obsessive desire for certain outcomes (e.g. personal gain, or success, or security) can lead to lies, deception and general loss of integrity (e.g. the fall itself; Abraham's lies re Sarah; the Gibeonites; the Amalekite who claimed to have killed Saul; Gehazi; false prophets in general; Ananias and Sapphira).

As was said at Cape Town, the idolatry of success (including in Christian ministry) can lead to loss of integrity in the way statistical outcomes are claimed, manipulated or falsified.

> We cannot build the kingdom of the God of truth on foundations of dishonesty. Yet in our craving for "success" and "results" we are tempted to sacrifice our integrity, with distorted or exaggerated claims that amount to lies. Walking in the light, however, "consists in . . . righteousness and truth."[1]
>
> We call on all church and mission leaders to resist the temptation to be less than totally truthful in presenting our

---

1. Eph 5:10.

work. We are dishonest when we exaggerate our reports with unsubstantiated statistics, or twist the truth for the sake of gain. We pray for a cleansing wave of honesty and the end of such distortion, manipulation and exaggeration. We call on all who fund spiritual work not to make unrealistic demands for measurable and visible results, beyond the need for proper accountability. Let us strive for a culture of full integrity and transparency. We will choose to walk in the light and truth of God, for the Lord tests the heart and is pleased with integrity.[2] (CTC IIE.4)[3]

However, setting aside for the moment such wrong and sinful obsession with outcomes, and focusing on a legitimate concern to pay proper and justified attention to the outcomes of our sincere efforts for the kingdom of God, what can we say about the outcomes of theological education in the light of the Bible?

2. The Outcomes of Theological Education (According to the Bible)

I believe we can affirm that TE, as we call it today – in its many different shapes (which we shall consider this week: formal, non-formal, etc.) – is a dimension of the biblical category of *teaching* as it has developed within the post-biblical history of the church.

What is the fundamental purpose of theological education? What is it we are trying to do?

To answer that question biblically, we have to ask further questions:

Who is TE for? Biblical answer: for the church – to serve the life, growth and mission of God's people, both in training their pastors and leaders, and in helping *all* believers to "be transformed through the renewal of their minds" (Rom 12:2) – to have "the mindset of the Spirit."

But *for what* does the church exist? Biblical answer: in the present era, for the sake of participating in the mission of God in the world. Therefore, *TE must serve the church in its mission.*

---

2. 1 Chr 29:17.

3. The Lausanne Movement, "The Cape Town Commitment" (2011), https://www.lausanne.org/content/ctc/ctcommitment.

The Cape Town Commitment puts it thus: "The mission of the Church on earth is to serve the mission of God, and the mission of theological education is to strengthen and accompany the mission of the Church" (CTC IIF.4).

There is a basic chain of impact. We want to see

- TE strengthening the church,
- so that the church, under God, can impact and change the world.

That puts TE right in the middle of the spiritual battle that the mission of God is engaged in.

TE, then, is a highly *consequential/purposive* activity. (It needs to be when you think what it costs!) We invest in it because we believe it has the power to achieve outcomes we consider desirable and important for the life and health of the church.

Now, if we look in the Bible, we don't find formal TE as such, but we do find an extraordinary emphasis on *teaching*. The Bible affirms from very early on, and repeatedly in both Testaments, that God's people need teaching and teachers, and that they are vulnerable and endangered when teachers are either absent or false and unfaithful.

What, then, are the *intended outcomes* of faithful and effective teaching, according to the Bible?

I suggest three focal points, each one connected with a Bible character who either was commissioned to teach or commissioned others to do so. Here are three biblical outcomes of teaching:

a) Mission – In a World of Many Nations: The Abrahamic Outcome

> Abraham will surely become a great and powerful nation, and all nations on earth will be blessed through him. For I have chosen him, so that he will direct his children and his household after him to keep the way of the Lord by doing what is right and just, so that the Lord will bring about for Abraham what he has promised him. (Gen 18:18–19)

In a world going the way of Sodom and Gomorrah (18:20–21; 19; etc.), God wanted to create a community that would be different – not just religiously different, but morally and socially distinctive (committed to righteousness and justice). That is the reason why God chose and called Abraham (v. 19).

But why did God want such a community, chosen in Abraham and instructed by him? In order to fulfil God's promise to Abraham, that through him and his descendants all nations on earth would find blessing (v. 18, echoing, of course, Gen 12:3).

There is a universal and missional context here to the teaching mandate. And, significantly, this instruction to Abraham comes in Genesis – long before the giving of the law in Exodus. Already, however, the ethical content of the law ("righteousness and justice") is anticipated in the kind of teaching that Abraham was to give to his household after him. This in itself shows that teaching (and therefore TE) is never merely the imparting of cognitive knowledge, but is the shaping of character and behaviour. The language of "walking in the way of the LORD" is common across the Torah, the prophets, the Psalms and wisdom literature.

So the ethical purpose of teaching in Old Testament Israel is governed by the missional purpose behind Israel's existence in the first place.

In the midst of the nations, this nation is to be *taught* how to live as the redeemed people of God, ultimately for the sake of the nations, and as part of the mission of God for the nations.

TE is intrinsically missional, and therefore ought to be intentionally missional.

b) Monotheism – In a World of Many Gods: The Mosaic Outcome

There is a strong emphasis on teaching in Deuteronomy. God's word in its broadest sense (the knowledge of God's mighty acts along with the understanding of God's law) must be constantly taught to the people, the whole people, and every generation of the people.

Moses himself is repeatedly the one who teaches Israel the requirements of their covenant God (to be followed by the Levitical priests, Deut 33:10). The primary content of his teaching was that YHWH, God of Israel, was the one and only, the unique and universal God, besides whom there is no other. For that reason, the first and greatest commandment, as Jesus said, is to love that one whole single God with our one whole single self – with heart and soul and strength. That command is immediately followed by the necessity of teaching – teaching that is to apply to the personal realm (hands and foreheads), the family realm (the doorposts of the home) and the public arena (the "gate").

> Hear, O Israel: The LORD our God, the LORD is one. Love the LORD your God with all your heart and with all your soul and with all your strength. These commandments that I give you today are to be on your hearts. Impress them on your children. Talk about them when you sit at home and when you walk along the road, when you lie down and when you get up. Tie them as symbols on your hands and bind them on your foreheads. Write them on the doorframes of your houses and on your gates. (Deut 6:4–9)

Such teaching was necessary because of the ambient polytheistic culture. Monotheism, in its proper biblical sense (i.e. not just the arithmetical conviction about the singularity of deity, but the specific affirmation of the transcendent universality of YHWH, God of Israel), is not an easy faith to inculcate or sustain (as the rest of the Old Testament shows). But since it is the primary *truth* and primary *obligation* and primary *blessing* (knowing, loving and worshipping the one true creator and redeemer God), whatever threatens it must be vigorously resisted at any cost (and it was a severe cost: ask any of the prophets).

So the whole of Deuteronomy 4 is a sustained challenge to avoid idolatry, and the emphasis within the chapter on teaching is strong:

> See, *I have taught you* decrees and laws as the LORD my God commanded me, so that you may follow them in the land you are entering to take possession of it. Observe them carefully, for this will show your wisdom and understanding to the nations, who will hear about all these decrees and say, "Surely this great nation is a wise and understanding people." What other nation is so great as to have their gods near them the way the LORD our God is near us whenever we pray to him? And what other nation is so great as to have such righteous decrees and laws as this body of laws I am setting before you today?
>
> Only be careful, and watch yourselves closely so that you do not forget the things your eyes have seen or let them fade from your heart as long as you live. *Teach them to your children* and to

their children after them. Remember the day you stood before the LORD your God at Horeb, when he said to me, "Assemble the people before me to hear my words so that they may learn to revere me as long as they live in the land and may *teach them to their children*." You came near and stood at the foot of the mountain while it blazed with fire to the very heavens, with black clouds and deep darkness. Then the LORD spoke to you out of the fire. You heard the sound of words but saw no form; there was only a voice. He declared to you his covenant, the Ten Commandments, which he commanded you to follow and then wrote them on two stone tablets. And *the LORD directed me at that time to teach you* the decrees and laws you are to follow in the land that you are crossing the Jordan to possess.

You saw no form of any kind the day the LORD spoke to you at Horeb out of the fire. Therefore watch yourselves very carefully, so that you do not become corrupt and make for yourselves an idol . . .

You were shown these things so that you might know that the LORD is God; besides him there is no other . . .

Acknowledge and take to heart this day that the LORD is God in heaven above and on the earth below. There is no other. Keep his decrees and commands, which I am giving you today, so that it may go well with you and your children after you and that you may live long in the land the LORD your God gives you for all time. (Deut 4:5–16, 35, 39–40; emphasis added)

If Israel were to be true to their mission among the nations, they must preserve the knowledge and worship of YHWH alone. For that reason, there must be teaching from generation to generation of all that God had done and all that God had said. Such should surely also be the ultimate aim and the core content of TE in our day.

c) Maturity – In a World of Many Falsehoods: The Pauline Outcome

When we talk about church growth, we usually mean numerical growth through successful evangelism and church planting. But if you had asked the apostle Paul, "Are your churches growing?," I think he would not have understood the question in that way. For Paul, evangelistic growth was just that – "gospel growth." So he could write, "*the gospel is bearing fruit and growing* throughout the whole world – just as it has been doing among you since the day you heard it and truly understood God's grace" (Col 1:6).

The kind of church growth Paul prayed for was growth in maturity. Here's how Paul described that kind of qualitative church growth: "We continually ask God to fill you with the knowledge of his will through all the wisdom and understanding that the Spirit gives, so that you may live a life worthy of the Lord and please him in every way: bearing fruit in every good work, growing in the knowledge of God, being strengthened with all power according to his glorious might so that you may have great endurance and patience" (Col 1:9–11). Paul wants the believers in Colossae to know God's story (the will and purpose of God), to live by God's standards and to prove God's strength. So for Paul, growth in maturity could be measured by (1) increasing knowledge and understanding of the faith, (2) a quality of living that was ethically consistent with the gospel and pleasing to God, and (3) perseverance under suffering and persecution.

But how will such Christian maturity be attained? Not surprisingly, through sound teaching by those whom Christ has gifted to the church. We could go to the Pastoral Epistles and prove this point repeatedly through the many places where Paul instructs Timothy and Titus to be teachers themselves, and trainers of teachers, and teachers of their people – all with a view to opposing false teachings and practices of all kinds. Then as now, believers were surrounded by competing worldviews and seductive alternatives to the true confession of faith. Then as now, sound teaching rooted in the Scriptures was the apostolic remedy and protection. But the point is made at its most succinct in Ephesians, and it is simply this: the teaching ministry within the church (within which we must include TE) is a Christ-ordained gifting; it is not an end in itself (the temptation of academia, itself one of the idolatrous seductions), but a means to an end, namely the equipping of God's own people for spiritual maturity and effective mission in the world:

> So Christ himself gave the apostles, the prophets, the evangelists, the pastors and teachers, to equip his people for works of service, so that the body of Christ may be built up until we all reach unity in the faith and in the knowledge of the Son of God and become mature, attaining to the whole measure of the fullness of Christ.
>
> Then we will no longer be infants, tossed back and forth by the waves, and blown here and there by every wind of teaching and by the cunning and craftiness of people in their deceitful scheming. Instead, speaking the truth in love, we will grow to become in every respect the mature body of him who is the head, that is, Christ. From him the whole body, joined and held together by every supporting ligament, grows and builds itself up in love, as each part does its work. (Eph 4:11–16)

To summarize then (and doubtless much more could be added as biblical outcomes of teaching), God has ordained that there should be teachers and teaching within the people of God,

1. So that they should be a community fit for participation in God's own mission to bring blessing to the nations;
2. So that they should remain committed to the one true God revealed in the Bible (as YHWH in Old Testament Israel, and incarnate in Jesus of Nazareth in the New Testament), and resist all the ambient idolatries of their cultures, and
3. So that they should grow to maturity in the understanding, the obedience and the endurance of faith.

The question we have to ask at this point is this: What kinds of graduates would we need to be turning out if we wished to show that our TE is being effective and fulfilling its biblical purpose – that is, the purposes for which God has ordained and provided for the teaching ministry among his people?

Surely it means that we ought to be seeing men and women who graduate and go out into their ministry

- *committed to mission* (in all its multiple biblical dimensions): eager to participate with God in his mission and to lead the communities they serve in the mission entrusted to the church.
- *faithful to biblical monotheism*: totally committed to the God of the Bible alone, and able to discern and resist the false gods that surround us. This includes not only the ability to understand and defend the uniqueness of Christ in contexts of religious plurality (and, where necessary, to bear costly witness to that faith), but also the discernment of many idolatries that are more subtle in all cultures (e.g. consumerism, ethnocentrism, etc.).
- *marked by maturity* in understanding, ethics and perseverance: able to do the things Paul urges Timothy and Titus to do; men and women who are taking care of their lives and their doctrine, and building up others in maturity, by godly example and steady biblical teaching.

So, first of all, is that indeed the kind of *goal* we have in mind as we shape our curricula, construct our syllabi, develop our lecture courses and hold our seminars and workshops? Are we *aiming* to produce people who are *biblically mission-minded, biblically monotheistic,* and *biblically mature*? (I use the word "biblically" in that sentence in the sense of "in accordance with the way the Bible defines and describes those three concepts.") And, second, are we being *effective* in producing such graduates, and how can we find out whether we are or not?

If this conference can help us at least face up to such questions, and work together to find appropriate methods of answering them, it will have helped us along a route that the Bible certainly wants us to walk in.

3. Planning for Effectiveness and Impact

Having established that, in biblical perspective, outcomes do matter to God, and that the outcomes of teaching/TE among God's people are such as we have just outlined, is there also biblical warrant for *planning* in order to achieve the kinds of outcomes, impact and effectiveness that are in line with God's purposes for the church and the world?

It does not take long, I think, to answer that question with a strong affirmative and to illustrate it with many examples from the Bible.

- Moses was clearly a planner, though not always from his own initiative: his father-in-law and the Spirit of the LORD needed to prompt him at times (Exod 18; Num 11).
- Jehoshaphat wanted to reform the nation, so he planned thoroughly and briefed those who were responsible to carry it out (2 Chr 19).
- Nehemiah planned, provided for, prepared and protected his great project.
- Ezra made good plans for the first ever program of Bible translation, accompanied by theological education by extension (Neh 8).
- The wisdom literature advocates prudence and planning, within a framework of trust in God's overruling providence and sovereignty.
- If Jesus knew that the ultimate goal of his incarnation, death and resurrection as Israel's Messiah would be mission to all nations, in fulfilment of the Scriptures (and his teaching in Luke 24 indicates that he did), then his three-year earthly ministry could be viewed as a very thorough planning and preparation for those to whom he entrusted the first phase of that mission.
- Paul clearly had plans (though he knew that the Spirit of Jesus could overrule them, and he was responsive to the "man from Macedonia" and the serendipitous meeting of a Jewish business woman by a European riverside on a Sabbath morning). The most obvious account of Paul's planning is found in Romans 15, with his sense of the conclusion of his mission in the eastern Mediterranean and his plans to go to Spain via Rome. How ironic it is that we don't know if Paul ever fulfilled that plan, but we would not have the letter to the Romans if he had not planned it. We owe his other letters to church-planting missions he had actually accomplished. We owe his greatest letter to a mission he *planned* but may never have accomplished.
- And there is clearly expressed intentionality behind his plans in the commissions he gave to Timothy in Ephesus and Titus in Crete.

So *should* we be planning? Yes, the Bible gives us encouragement to do our planning in order to achieve effectiveness and impact.

But *what* exactly should we be planning in TE as such that will achieve the kinds of impacts we described above – men and women committed to biblical mission, monotheism and maturity? Doubtless we will consider many good and important proposals this week to strengthen our effectiveness in achieving those goals. But, in my opinion, nothing will contribute more to the goal of sending out graduates who will be effective in those terms than a re-centring of the Bible itself at the heart of the whole living organism of TE with its many arms and legs and streams and branches (to mix metaphors shamelessly).

This is something you have heard me call for before at ICETE (International Commission on Evangelical Theological Education): *a biblical and missional reorientation and reintegration of the whole TE enterprise,* including radical auditing of our curricula at macro and micro levels.

The Cape Town Commitment quite emphatically calls for this twice:

> We long to see a fresh conviction, gripping all God's Church, of the central necessity of Bible teaching for the Church's growth in ministry, unity and maturity. (CTC IID.1.d.1)

> We long that all church planters and theological educators should place the Bible at the centre of their partnership, not just in doctrinal statements but in practice. Evangelists must use the Bible as the supreme source of the content and authority of their message. Theological educators must re-centre the study of the Bible as the core discipline in Christian theology, integrating and permeating all other fields of study and application. Above all theological education must serve to equip pastor-teachers for their prime responsibility of preaching and teaching the Bible. (CTC IIF.4.d)

So,

- If we want to see those who lead the church in every generation characterized by a passion for the mission of God as the Bible reveals it, and enthusiastically leading their people to participate with God in multiple and effective ways in their own contexts;
- If we want to see them follow in the footsteps of the prophets and apostles in affirming and defending the biblical revelation of the one

living God and of his Son, Jesus Christ, as the only Saviour and Lord, and able to discern and resist the idolatries that entice their people;

- If we want to see them exhibiting the marks of biblical maturity, in their lives and character, in the Christlike quality of their leadership and in the effectiveness of their teaching and preaching;

- *Then surely nothing will contribute more to the effective achievement of those outcomes than to regard the Bible itself as the "main thing," and to keep the main thing the main thing, within an integrated curriculum that injects biblical thinking, biblical questions, biblical criteria, the biblical grand narrative, into every discipline – including Biblical Studies itself.*

If we want better biblical outputs, we need better biblical inputs.

I think this means, for example, that teachers of *systematic theology* seek to show how the grand house of Christian theology in fact reflects the implications of every part of the revelation contained within the great Bible story.

It means that *church history* is seen as the outworking of God's mission in "Act 5" of the Bible story – and is assessed in terms of its faithfulness or

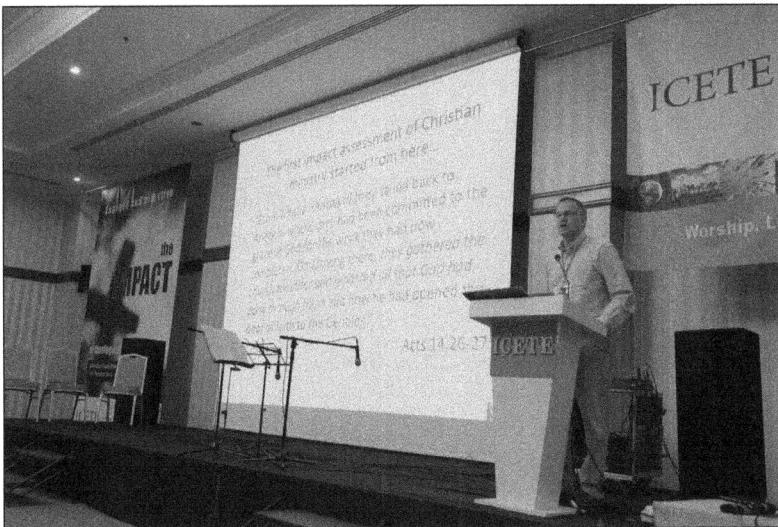

Dr Chris Wright

otherwise to the patterns already set in "Acts 1–4" and the expectation of "Act 6."[4]

It means that in *ethics* we help students not merely to weigh up the different systems of ethics (whether theological, philosophical or ethical), but to bring every ethical issue into the light of every part of the Bible story – light that is shed on the issue by the implications of the great facts and truths of each section, all six acts.

We are tempted to multiply the number of *bolt-on courses* on this or that new issue that has just arisen in the world. Something else becomes "a big issue," and we feel we must add a course on it to our already over-burdened curriculum, often squeezing out the biblical courses to make room. But, of course, as soon as the students graduate and leave college some other "big issue" will hit them. Now they are stumped because they didn't "take a course in that subject at seminary," and so they lose their effectiveness, relevance and impact. Rather, we need to teach people how to *think biblically* about any and every issue that will arise. They need to have learned how to bring every issue into the light of all the key points along the Bible narrative and how to hear the major "voices" of the biblical canon. The Bible may not have a direct answer (chapter and verse) to the new problem, but systematically shining the light of biblical revelation along the whole sweep of the canon on to the issue will help generate a response that can have some claim to being "biblical."

I would love to see such a "whole-Bible approach" become characteristic of all theological education – across all disciplines. We should be learning together to read the Bible as a whole and to root our theology and our practice deeply in the "whole counsel of God."

We need to help our students see that the Bible is not just an *object* of their study (one item among many on their list of "courses," limited to when they are doing "Biblical Studies"), but the *subject* of their thinking – about everything. That is to say, the Bible is not just something we "think about," but rather something we "think with." The Bible informs and guides the way we

---

4. See C. Bartholomew and M. Goheen, *The Drama of Scripture: Finding Our Place in the Biblical Story*, 2nd ed. (Grand Rapids: Baker, 2014). They present the whole Bible story as the drama of the mission of God, a drama in six acts: Act 1, Creation; Act 2, the Fall (human rebellion); Act 3, God's Promise to Abraham and the OT Story; Act 4, the Gospel of Christ; Act 5, the Mission of the Church to the Nations; Act 6, the New Creation.

think about everything else – whether in the classroom or in all the rest of life in the world. The Bible is the lens through which all of life, including all that we learn in seminary, is seen and assessed.

So, to be very frank at this point, whenever theological education neglects or marginalizes the teaching of the Bible, or squeezes it to the edges of a curriculum that has become crammed with other things, then such TE has itself become unbiblical and disobedient to the clear mandate that we find taught and modelled in both Testaments. Theological education which does not produce men and women who know their Bibles thoroughly, who know how to teach and preach the Scriptures, who are able to think biblically through any and every issue they confront, and who are able to feed and strengthen God's people with God's Word – whatever else such theological education may do, or claim, or be accredited for, *it is failing the church by failing to equip the church and its leaders to fulfil their calling and mission in the world.*

So my plea is simply this: if we are considering how to plan for our TE to be effective and make an impact in ways that matter most to God *according to the Bible*, let us allow the Bible itself to be the primary integrating lens through which we educate our students for everything else. Can we plan to *that* end?

4. Proving Effectiveness and Impact: Can We Measure Them?

It is one thing to invest time and effort in *planning* to be effective in the long-term impact of our TE, but can we *prove* that we are? This is of course much more complex and ambiguous.

The Biblical Warrant

The Bible is not at all reluctant to describe and quantify *successful outcomes* in all kinds of ways, with facts and figures to prove the point. We are told, for example, the details of all the precious materials given for the construction of the tabernacle (Exod 35), and of the tribal offerings when it was complete (Num 7). Likewise, David's appeal for gifts for the temple meets with a very successful outcome, duly recorded (1 Chr 28–29). We are regularly told the size of enemy armies and the scale of military success, proving the power of God in victory. Samson kills a thousand Philistines with the jaw-bone of a donkey, "making an impact," one might say, at least from the Philistines' point of view.

The Gospels portray the outcomes of Jesus's word and actions, sometimes numerically – proving who he was and why he had come. Likewise, Acts records the expanding numbers of new believers, and proves the effectiveness and impact of the gospel in Ephesus in terms of an economic downturn in the idol industry and the ensuing riot. One might say that John's vision in Revelation of a great multitude from every tribe and nation and language and people is the ultimate proof of the outcome of God's promise to Abraham in Genesis. The whole Bible is one great "outcome and impact" story!

Biblical Warnings

Counting and measuring, however, can be ambiguous or dangerous. The spies brought back fruit that was enormous, demonstrating the verifiable goodness of the land God had promised. But ten of them had measured the size of the "giants" in the land and the height of the walls of the cities – and felt like "grasshoppers" in comparison. So a promise, an opportunity and a whole generation were squandered by deceptive measurements and an inferiority complex.

David's motive in counting the size of his armed forces is not made explicit, but it was against the advice of his senior commander, Joab, and it displeased the Lord. Presumably it was a sign of *pride or self-sufficiency*, as if the security of his kingdom depended on the size of his army, rather than on the promise of his God. The results were tragic (1 Chr 21).

Being over-concerned with measurable results can lead to *boasting* – a temptation Paul was aware of and resisted. He would personally boast of nothing, except what he could tell of God's accomplishments: "Therefore I glory in Christ Jesus in my service to God. I will not venture to speak of anything except what Christ has accomplished through me in leading the Gentiles to obey God by what I have said and done – by the power of signs and wonders, through the power of the Spirit of God" (Rom 15:17–19). We need constantly to hem in our countings and claims with the prior and infinite reality of the grace of God.

Not to us, LORD, not to us
> but to your name be the glory,
> because of your love and faithfulness. (Ps 115:1)

So the Bible gives us both *warrant* for appropriate counting and measurement, and *warning* against doing so for wrong reasons or motives. Discernment is called for – and we will need to exercise it constantly throughout this conference.

Furthermore, let us keep in mind that there is that which is *immeasurable* – God himself, for example, as is obvious, and all the evidence of his love, grace and covenant commitment to us. The psalmists make the point often.

Many, LORD my God,
> are the wonders you have done,
> the things you planned for us.

None can compare with you;
> were I to speak and tell of your deeds,
> they would be too many to declare. (Ps 40:5)

The work of God is effective and makes an impact, but it is often way beyond any of our puny measurement tools.

We all know the saying that sometimes what really counts is uncountable (while what can be counted may not count for much). We also need to say that outcomes are not only often uncountable, but they are often also *unpredictable*. It is God who is sovereign, and God's Spirit "blows where he wills." The wisdom of Ecclesiastes might form a useful and sobering background music to all that we attempt here this week. In all our efforts to ensure good outcomes and to measure our impact, let us remember that there are things we do not and cannot know in advance, and can neither control nor predict. So a great deal of faith is needed, along with courage and a spirit of adventure.

Ship your grain across the sea;
> after many days you may receive a return.

Invest in seven ventures, yes, in eight;
> you do not know what disaster may come upon the land.

If clouds are full of water,
> they pour rain on the earth.

Whether a tree falls to the south or to the north,
in the place where it falls, there it will lie.
Whoever watches the wind will not plant;
whoever looks at the clouds will not reap.

As you do not know the path of the wind,
or how the body is formed in a mother's womb,
so you cannot understand the work of God,
the Maker of all things.

Sow your seed in the morning,
and at evening let your hands not be idle,
for you do not know which will succeed,
whether this or that,
or whether both will do equally well. (Eccl 11:1–6)

Finally, I would plead that in the midst of our legitimate concern to count and measure and verify our effectiveness and impact, we *do not neglect the power of testimony and story*. The Bible, surely, provides plenty of both. We have masses of facts, quantities and numbers – plenty of them in both Testaments – showing us we are not wrong to engage with that dimension of our task. But just imagine if the Gospels, or the book of Acts, were given to us solely in the form of numbers – as they could be.

We could just insert some statistics into the Apostles' Creed!

Jesus
performed 127 miracles of healing
preached 29 sermons
told 31 parables
fed 9,000 people (at least)
etc.
The early church expanded by 3,000, then 5,000, etc.
The gospel reached 25 towns through Paul's missionary journeys, etc.

We could put the New Testament onto a few PowerPoint slides full of such statistics. But how poor we would be without the great story and all the little stories woven into it.

The Bible puts a lot of emphasis on the power of testimony, of the telling of what God has done. Indeed, it was by the telling and re-telling of those stories that the teaching of both Testaments was primarily accomplished – with the intended outcome that the community would be shaped and equipped by knowing the stories of God in action and constantly expecting God to "do it again."

All I am saying is, let us refrain from despising what is sometimes rather disparagingly called *"anecdotal evidence."* We certainly need to complement such evidence with facts and figures, percentages and graphs, and so on, where we can do so, but it is in the stories that the real story of the effectiveness and impact of our efforts will be heard, understood and remembered.

Or to put it simply: forty-five years ago, John Stott began the program now known as Langham Scholars. Has it been effective? you ask. Has it made an impact? Well, I could put the statistics on one PowerPoint slide right now – the number of scholars, the countries they serve, the numbers of seminaries in which they teach, the numbers of students they have taught and books they have written, the multiplication of ministries they have generated, and so on. And that is all useful information and we are gathering it very carefully. You might be impressed, but you would forget it by tomorrow.

I would much rather introduce you to the thirty-five-plus Langham Scholars who are here at ICETE 2015 and let them tell you their stories. That would be the evidence of lives, the power of testimony. That would be to see outcomes, impact and effectiveness *embodied* as well as measured.

So let us rejoice in the statistics whenever we can, for the Bible does. But let us rejoice even more in what our eyes have seen and our ears have heard.

Discussion Questions

1. As you consider the topic of "assessment," where you do find yourself on the suggested spectrum between "enthusiasm" and "suspicion"? What are one or two key factors that shape your attitude towards assessment?

2. The outcome of Theological Education as "the mission of God for the sake of the nations" is basic to the thrust of this chapter. Describe some ways in

which your school/program takes this outcome seriously. What are one or two ways in which you think your school/program could do better?

3. Several outcomes of theological education are suggested: (a) the Abrahamic outcome of being intentionally missional; (b) the Mosaic outcome of teaching from generation to generation all that God has done and all that God has said; and (c) the Pauline outcome of holistic maturity. Give rough percentages as to the proportional emphases in your own courses of study. What other emphases does your school/program include? Suggest one specific area in which you believe that your school/program might move towards a healthier balance between these emphases.

4. What do you understand by the "whole-Bible approach" to curriculum suggested in this chapter? What are some of the strengths of such an approach? What are some of the potential hazards?

5. As you approach the task of assessment, what did you personally find most helpful in the final cautionary section on field research through biblical eyes?

2

Assessment Beyond the 4Bs

Scott Cunningham
President, Overseas Council USA

B y "the 4B's," I refer to the framework we have often used to assess our seminaries: bricks, books, bucks and bodies. However, during our recent Overseas Council project focusing on outcomes-based curriculum development, I learned a different approach to assessment of our programs. In this chapter I'd like to share the basic outline of that learning, beginning with my encounter with what was being done by the Arab Baptist Theological Seminary (ABTS, located in Beirut, Lebanon) and how that influenced my understanding of a better way to assess our theological education programs.

Several years ago, ABTS had radically revised its curriculum in order to make it more responsive to the changing needs for church leadership in the Middle Eastern context. They were now ready to assess their experiment. As I heard their story, I came away with several new insights.

1. Changing the Focus of Assessment

The first thing that was significant about their evaluation was *the change in focus of what was being assessed.*

Instead of focusing on what the seminary was doing, *the focus was on the results* of what the seminary was doing. So emphasis was placed on assessing the actual outcomes of the curriculum. Where are the results of the curriculum seen? Ultimately, the results of the seminary are demonstrated in the ministries of the graduates and in the churches they serve. So this becomes the new focus of the assessment process.

This is a change in focus from the way that much of our assessment typically takes place. For many years, standards for seminary accreditation focused on:

- the resources of the school, such as the facilities, faculty, funds and library (hence, the 4 Bs); and
- the activities which take place inside the school, such as the curriculum, governance, policies and procedures.

However, if the mission of the seminary is to serve the church, the only way to know whether or not the seminary's mission is being accomplished is to ask, "How well are the churches where our graduates minister being served? What difference do our graduates make in those churches and in the other ministries that they lead?" In the words of Rupen Das, former ABTS faculty member: "Whether a theological institution has been successful is measured by whether its graduates are effective in their place of ministry."

What ABTS was doing became an exciting and important case study for me. For us as a community of theological educators and leaders, this approach to assessment has been our expressed desire and our ambition for many years. Yet I've seen very little progress in this direction as I look at how assessment is actually practised.

This desire, for instance, is stated in the important statement "The ICETE Manifesto on the Renewal of Evangelical Theological Education," which says:

5. Continuous Assessment:

. . . we must accept it as a duty, and not merely as beneficial, to discern and evaluate the *results* of our programmes, so that there may be a valid basis for judging the degree to which intentions are being achieved. This requires that we institute means for reviewing the *actual performance of our graduates* in relation to our stated objectives.[1]

---

1. ICETE, "ICETE Manifesto on the Renewal of Evangelical Theological Education," http://www.icete-edu.org/manifesto/; emphasis added.

2. Applying the Logic Model

The second most important feature of this new approach – the change of focus from what was happening in the seminary (resources and the curriculum) to the results – was the conceptual framework used for this assessment. The "logic model" (or the "theory of change") is commonly used in the world of non-profit or community development, where the success or achievement of an organization cannot be measured in terms of monetary profit or the financial bottom line.

What Is the "Logic Model"?

The "logic model" is "a programme theory [which] explains how an intervention (a project, a programme, a policy, a strategy) is understood to contribute to a chain of results that produce the intended or actual impacts."[2]

To illustrate, we can take an example from the sphere of community development. Imagine that children in a particular village are dying from unclean water. You want to assess an educational program which was designed and implemented to address this problem. Was this program successful? Did it accomplish its mission?

What We Do and the Results of What We Do

The "logic model" says you look at the program in two main parts: what you do and the results of what you do. What you do is also broken down into two parts: the *input* and the *activities*. Similarly, the "results of what you do" is broken down into two (or sometimes three) parts: the *output* and the *outcomes/impact*:

- *Activities:* what the program does to fulfil its mission.
- *Input:* resources needed to carry out activities.
- *Output:* the immediate, short-term result of the activities. The goods or services produced, or people trained.
- *Outcomes and Impact:* the medium- and long-term results that are the consequence of the output.

---

2. "Develop Programme Theory," BetterEvaluation, accessed 20 September 2017, http://www.betterevaluation.org/en/plan/define/develop_logic_model.

An Example

We can now apply the logic model to assess the community development educational program we are using as an illustration.

We first determine the indicators of the success of the educational program. We could identify the following to assess the *activities* of the project:

- How many mothers were taught about clean water?
- What was the content of what was taught to the mothers about clean water?

So one possible indicator of success of the project, looking at activities, could be that 90 percent of mothers in the village were taught about clean water.

If we were assessing the *input*, what would be an indicator that our program was successful?

- How much money was spent in the program?
- Were the instructors qualified to teach in the program?

So one possible indicator focusing on input could be that $10,000 were spent on the project; or the instructors were trained for ten hours on how to use the curriculum on clean water.

If we were assessing the *output*, what would be an indicator that our program was successful?

- We could test the knowledge, skills and attitudes of the mothers after the training program compared to before the training.

Using this approach, one possible indicator of success could be that mothers who were trained now believe that clean water is important for the health of their children. Also, mothers know how to boil water to purify it.

If we were assessing the *outcomes/impact*, what would be an indicator that our program was successful? Several possible indicators come to mind: 90 percent of families whose mothers were trained boil their drinking water for at least ten minutes. Or the infant mortality rate in the village where mothers are trained (i.e. how many children live beyond their first birthday) has decreased by 50 percent compared to the rate experienced before the program.

If you participated in this program (that is, you designed it, funded it, directed it or taught in it), which of these indicators is going to be the most important to you? Which indicator best demonstrates the success of the project? What is it that you really want to assess? The activities, the input, the output or the outcomes and impact?

Ultimately, you're not so interested in the *input* or *activities*. Ultimately, it doesn't really matter how many mothers were trained, or how many learned that water purification was connected to their children's health. It's possible that the whole village could have been trained without any discernable difference in achieving what the project was really intended to achieve. Ultimately, it's not the indicators of what you do that it is important to assess; instead, you're really interested in the *results* of what you do. Ultimately, the success of the project is measured by the indicators of the *outcomes* and *impact* – how the program makes a difference and accomplishes the mission. So, in our community development illustration, the real success of the training project can be measured only by measuring the reduction in infant mortality.

The point of the illustration is that ultimately the success of our educational endeavours is measured not by what we do, but by the results of what we do.

3. Applying the Logic Model to Seminary Education

We can now apply the logic model to the assessment of a theological education program.

We start with the same framework:

Activities

For education, this is the "curriculum" broadly defined. Possible indicators are:
- How many credit hours are required to earn a bachelor's degree?
- How many courses are in Bible or in theology?

Input (or Resources)

- How many faculty have earned doctorates?
- Here we include the four "Bs" which are typically measured: bricks (referring to buildings), bucks (funding), books (in the library) and bodies (number and quality of students and faculty)

Output

- What are the character, knowledge, skills as seen in the graduate? (What we desire to see as an output from our seminary is sometimes expressed in a "graduate profile.")

Outcomes (and Impact)

- These are the changes that are the intended result of our programs, which are seen in the performance of our graduates in the places in which they serve.
- Ultimately, this is seen in the spiritual growth of the church. This is the desired result of our theological education program.

Note that what is often called *outcomes-based education* by educators is, in our framework, actually focused on output, and would thus be more accurately described as *output-based* education.

In summary:

- *Input* and *Activities* focus on the *school* itself. This has been the usual focus of accreditation in the past and still often is today.
- *Output* focuses on the *graduate*. Sometimes our assessment even extends to the graduate.
- *Outcomes* focus on the *churches* as the places where the graduates serve. It asks the question, "What are the characteristics of a healthy church in this context?" and "To what extent are our graduates affecting health in the church?"

Conclusion: Three Things I Learned

Let me conclude by pointing out the three most important things I learned from my experience with ABTS and our subsequent Overseas Council project regarding the assessment of our theological education programs.

a) *Changing focus.* This approach shifts the focus of assessment from what we do in the school to the results of what we do as seen in the graduates and their churches. One could say that it shifts our focus from the "bucks, bricks, books and bodies" to the "bang," that is, the outcomes and impact.

b) *Applying the logic model.* Not only does this approach help us to focus on the results, but it also helps us distinguish between different levels of results: that is, between the output (as seen in the learning of the student) and the outcomes and impact (as seen in the graduate and in his or her ministry in the church).

c) *Improving the curriculum.* It is only if we can assess the degree to which we are achieving the purpose of our programs that we can then ask, "How can we use what we have learned from this assessment to make adjustments in our programs/activities to make improvements?" This is why we called our project "Research-Driven Curriculum Revision." That is, our assessment is not for the sake of assessment itself, but as a way to improve our program by providing data which indicates the results.

During the last year and a half, Overseas Council walked with ten seminaries from around the world learning together about how to assess their programs. It has been a privilege to see them work with these concepts, and learn and develop new ways of envisioning their schools.

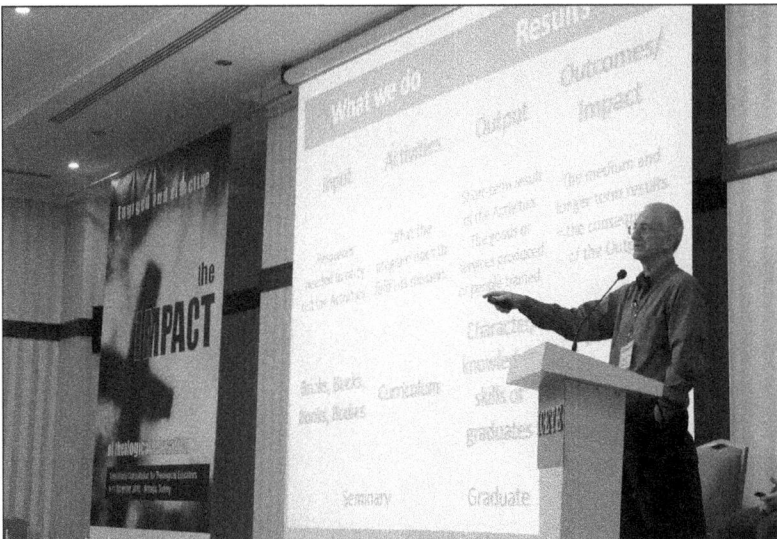

Discussion Questions

1. How well are the churches being served where our graduates minister? What difference do our graduates make in those churches and in other ministries that they lead?

For these questions to be meaningful they need greater specificity. For your school, how would you go about defining the meaning of "difference"?

What do you think are some of the main criteria for establishing whether your graduates are fulfilling the school's purpose? Who should be involved in determining these criteria?

2. A key to using the "logic model" for assessment is the ultimate goal of impact. Looking at the local context of the churches where your graduates serve, make a list of at least three major areas where you long to see meaningful impact in the community. Please be as specific as possible. How would you go about assessing change in these areas?

3

Connecting Curriculum and Context:

The Foundations for Relevance in Theological Education[1]

Rupen Das
National Director, Canadian Bible Society

Today, as we meet in Antalya, it is very appropriate that we are discussing the relevance and impact of theological education in a part of the world where being faithful to the teachings of the apostles in a context of competing philosophies and allegiances was a significant challenge for the very early church. The question was, how was the truth about Christ communicated in contexts that were very different from the Jewish world where the apostles had known Christ? The issue was one of connecting the teachings of Jesus and the apostles with context.

This challenge was probably most clearly seen in the life of Polycarp, whose family had moved from Jerusalem after its fall in AD 70 and had settled in the province of Asia, a few hundred kilometres west of here. It was here as a young man, in the city of Ephesus, that he was discipled by the apostle John. Polycarp was later appointed by John himself as Bishop of Smyrna, present-day Izmir, further up the coast.

---

1. The chapter has been expanded and published under the same title by Langham. Rupen Das, *Connecting Curriculum with Context*, ICETE Series (Carlisle, UK: Langham Global Library, 2015).

The importance of Polycarp is that he was one of the few church fathers who were a direct link between the apostles, who had known Jesus and heard his teachings, and the early church of the late first century and early second century. At a time before the young church's doctrines had been crystalized through the various councils and creeds, the challenge for Polycarp was to ensure that the teachings of the apostles that he had heard directly from John remained unadulterated and were passed on to the next generation.

This was no easy task. Hellenism was on the rise and a Greek worldview dominated any intelligent discourse. The apostle John had been able to contextualize the understanding of who Christ is by adopting the term *Logos* from Greek philosophy to try to explain how God is involved in the world and in human life. Observing John's effort at contextualization, Polycarp had learnt not only the doctrines that were beginning to define this new faith, but also how to connect the reality of Christ, whom he had come to know, with the cultural and intellectual context in which he lived.

This proved critical when he was confronted with the heretic Marcion, who tried to separate the church from its Jewish roots and in the process redefine who Jesus and God were. In order to deal with the heresy, Polycarp was able to sift through the arguments from Greek culture and philosophy that undergirded Marcion's heresy and did not align with the truth, and, in the process, ensure that the early church remained rooted in the teachings of Jesus and the apostles.

This, then, is the challenge that all theologians and missiologists face: how does one take truth learnt in one context and make it relevant in another? Princeton theologian Daniel Migliore writes, "Confession of Jesus Christ takes place in particular historical and cultural contexts. Our response to the questions of who we say Jesus Christ is and how he helps us is shaped in important ways by the particular context in which these questions arise."[2] For theological educators, the challenge is even more complex: how does one teach students the skills to take the Christ they know in their context and enable people in a different historical and cultural context to encounter the same Christ? This is exactly what the apostle John had to do: to take the Christ

---

2. Daniel Migliore, *Faith Seeking Understanding: An Introduction to Christian Theology* (Grand Rapids, MI: Eerdmans, 2004).

whom he had known in a Jewish Palestinian context and teach Polycarp in an intellectually Greek and politically Roman context how to proclaim Christ. In a sense, the apostle John's effectiveness in discipling and training Polycarp can be assessed by the success with which Polycarp handled the Marcion heresy.

Assessment of the impact of theological education has always been a challenge. What we are looking at is how we connect the theological education we provide with the contexts where our students will be ministering in order for them to be effective. In a pluralistic world with greatly differing contexts and cultures in which our graduates are ministering, theological education has to be context-sensitive and -relevant. It is no longer enough to ensure that students have mastered a core of theological concepts and truths, and have biblical knowledge and some basic ministry skills. The impact of a theological institution is measured by the effectiveness of its graduates in their specific ministry contexts. Therefore the theological curriculum has to be connected with the contexts of the graduates.

Pastor and theologian Eugene Peterson states that all ministry is rooted in geography. He writes, "Now is the time to rediscover the meaning of the local, and in terms of church, the parish. All churches are local. All pastoral work takes place geographically."[3] If this is true, do the graduates have the ability and the tools to understand the local context?

Others at this conference will be looking at how one assesses the effectiveness of theological education and its impact. This morning I will try to lay some foundations for that discussion by looking at (1) how different models of theological education over time evolved to respond to needs within the church and in society, and (2) how a theological institution intentionally connects with its context. I will present a model of how that is done.

Models of Theological Education

There is no one model of theological education. From the time of the early church to the present, the type of theological education available has been based

---

3. Eugene Peterson, *Under the Unpredictable Plant: An Exploration in Vocational Holiness* (Grand Rapids, MI: Eerdmans, 1994).

on (1) the needs of the church in a particular context and (2) the influence of the local culture.

There are three commonly accepted models of theological education. The original thinking was developed by David Kelsey of Yale Divinity School describing a classical versus a vocational approach.[4] To this was added Robert Banks's missional approach.[5]

The classical model, sometimes referred to as the "Athens," defined theological education as Christian character formation or *paideia*. It was derived from classical Greek educational methodology and the term literally means child-rearing or education. It is a process of moulding character. The objective was to produce well-rounded and fully educated citizens.[6] The concept of *paideia* does not start with the individual person and his or her potential but with the concept of the ideal person. So the process of education was to educate and mould human beings into the ideal man who represented human nature in its truest form. Greek and Roman philosophers, artists, sculptors, educators and poets drew their inspiration from the concept of an ideal man. The goal of classical education was the transformation of the individual.

The early church adopted and then adapted this model. Some of the church fathers saw the Christian faith as a form of *paideia*: in order to grow in one's faith, one's character had to be formed. By the medieval and monastic period it had become the dominant educational philosophy. *Paideia* influenced Basil of Caesarea in the development of his monastic rules.[7] The objective was to enable individuals to develop a holistic vision that understood and grasped the totality of life, including the world. Rather than just knowing about God, the focus was on knowing God.

Brian Edgar at Asbury Theological Seminary writes, "It is not about *theology*, that is, the formal study of the *knowledge* of God, but it is more

---

4. David H. Kelsey, *Between Athens and Berlin: The Theological Debate* (Grand Rapids, MI: Eerdmans, 1993), 27.

5. Robert Banks, *Reenvisioning Theological Education* (Grand Rapids, MI: Eerdmans, 1999).

6. Richard Tarnas, *The Passion of the Western Mind: Understanding the Ideas That Have Shaped Our World View* (New York: Harmony, 1993), 29–30.

7. Werner Jaeger, *Early Christianity and Greek Paideia* (Cambridge, MA: Harvard University Press, 1961), 90. St Basil's Wider and Shorter Rules became the model for Eastern monasticism from the fifth century onwards. They influenced the development of the monastic orders established by St Benedict of Norcia, St Dominic and St Francis of Assisi.

about what Kelsey calls *theologia*, that is gaining the wisdom of God."[8] The emphasis was on holiness and the transformation of the individual. Edgar states that in this model of theological education, holiness and moral and spiritual transformation are central.

The vocational model, referred to as the "Berlin" and with its roots in the Enlightenment, sees theological education as being a preparation for a professional Christian vocation and therefore needing to be situated within the context of a university as an academic discipline. The German term *Wissenschaft* means a study or science that requires systematic research. The origin of *Wissenschaft* as a model for seminaries is Friedrich Schleiermacher's pioneering work at Humboldt University in Berlin. The goal was no longer the moral and personal formation of individuals through the study of authoritative texts, but training students in rigorous enquiry in order to move from theory to practical applications.

Schleiermacher's task was to design a curriculum that would train professional ministers for the state church in Germany, within the context of defending theology's status as an academic discipline. He built on the fourfold structure of the traditional theological curriculum from the period of the Reformation that was used to train pastors and teachers. This consisted of Biblical Studies, Church History, Dogmatics or Systematic Theology, and Practical Theology. He adapted it to a modern university context. Schleiermacher's argument was that the university had a mandate to train clergymen; their training was no different from that of the practitioners of medicine or law. In all three disciplines there was a progression from theory to professional practice.[9] Adopting this model of study came with the loss of *paideia* and of personal, moral and spiritual formation.

Schleiermacher's model is still very much the framework that is used in most theological training today, though the specific content of the four areas of study may have changed. There is an understanding that both knowledge and skills are needed for pastoral ministry. Many evangelical seminaries incorporate

---

8. Brian Edgar, "The Theology of Theological Education," *Evangelical Review of Theology* 29, no. 3 (2005): 210.

9. Friedrich Schleiermacher and Terrence Tice, *Brief Outline of Theology as a Field of Study: Revised Translation of the 1811 and 1830 Editions*, 3rd ed. (Louisville, KY: Westminster John Knox, 2011), 137.

elements of both classical and vocational models in their curriculum. There is an emphasis on character formation and the moulding of a worldview, as well as on the "professional studies" required to be a pastor or in some kind of Christian ministry, though the emphasis is more on theory and knowledge.

The last commonly accepted model, *the missional model*, was developed by Robert Banks at Macquarie University in Sydney and is referred to as the "Jerusalem." The missional model sees mission encompassing all aspects of life – family, friendships, work and neighbourhood. For Banks, mission is not just being mission-oriented but "an education undertaken with a view to what God is doing in the world, considered from a global perspective."[10] Therefore theological education is not an independent discipline but is seen as part of mission. The objective is to be involved in *missio Dei* – the mission of God. It's a model that provides a connection between action and reflection. For Banks, the best theological education and spiritual formation is partly field-based, stretches students to do what they are studying, encompasses all of life and addresses mission opportunities.

Thinking on the three categories has been further developed to incorporate other models of theological education. Brian Edgar, professor at Asbury Theological Seminary, adds a fourth model called *the confessional model*. Referred to as the "Geneva," it sees the goal of theological education as knowing God through the means of grace and the traditions in a particular faith community, and more specifically, through the creed and confession of that community. This involves "formation . . . through *in-formation* about the tradition and *en-culturation* with it."[11] This is done through teaching about the founders, the heroes, the struggles, the strengths and the traditions that are both distinctive and formative for that community. Examples of this are denominational-affiliated seminaries and training institutions of specific mission agencies.

---

10. Banks, *Reenvisioning*, 142.
11. Edgar, "Theology," 213.

Classical			Confessional
	GOAL ↓ transform the individual	GOAL ↓ knowing God	
Athens			Geneva
academy			seminary
	theologia	doxology	
	missiology	scientia	
Jerusalem	GOAL ↓ convert the world	GOAL ↓ strengthen the church	Berlin
community			university
Missional			Vocational

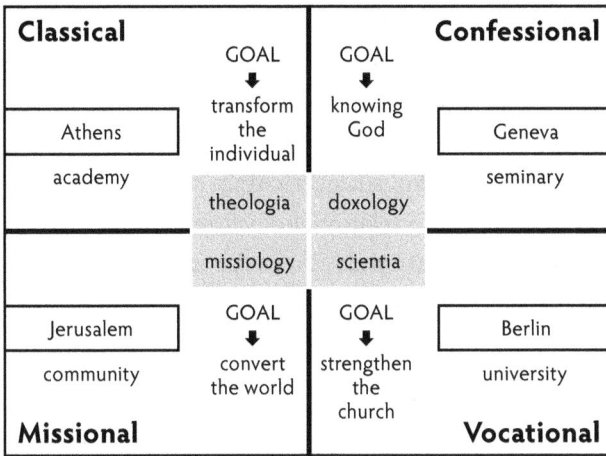

Figure 1: Four Models of Theological Education[12]

Darren Cronshaw, mission researcher at the Baptist Union of Victoria in Australia, adds two further models.[13] The first is *the contextual model* and is referred to as "Auburn." According to Cronshaw, theology and mission need to be expressed in specific contexts such as those in his local neighbourhood of Auburn.[14] So theological training for the contextual model deals with understanding local context and learning how to build community (*koinonia*). It is this community that lives out the gospel, and in the process the boundaries dissolve. Together they experience community and demonstrate the love of God so that others may belong, and one day believe.[15]

The final model that Cronshaw adds is *the spiritual model*, also known as "New Delhi." This is a model for a multicultural and pluralistic world. Cronshaw writes,

> A New Delhi context for missional spirituality is the ashram. As the balance of global power and Christian influence is shifting to the Global South, Kraig Klaudt artfully suggests that certain Indian

12. Adapted from Edgar, 213.

13. Darren Cronshaw, "Reenvisioning Theological Education and Missional Spirituality," *Journal of Adult Theological Education* 9, no. 1 (2012): 9–27.

14. John Franke, *The Character of Theology: An Introduction to Its Nature, Task, and Purpose* (Grand Rapids, MI: Baker Academic, 2005), 90.

15. Stuart Murray, *Church After Christendom* (Bletchley: Paternoster, 2005).

ashrams feature helpful characteristics that theological education can adopt. These ashrams are located "in the world" without fences; are open to all; offer community living that is engaged in service; emphasize simple living and spiritual maturity more than publishing; provide a holistic curriculum of intellectual, spiritual, political, aesthetic and relational development; and create time and space for spirituality and self-awareness. Locating theological education and missional spirituality in New Delhi reminds me to engage with the worldviews of my neighbours and to welcome the alternative model of the ashram.[16]

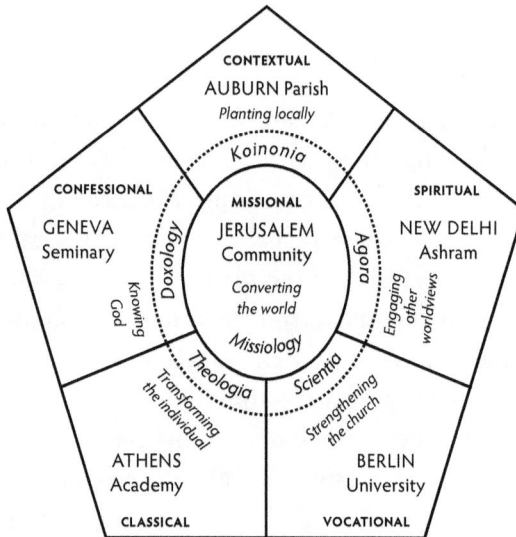

Figure 2: Six Models of Theological Education and Missional Spirituality[17]

Each of these models understands its role in theological formation differently, and as a result defines impact differently. While there is great value in each of these models, and certain elements of each model can be transferred across cultures and contexts, each of these six models of theological education responds to specific needs in the church and in society.

16. Cronshaw, "Reenvisioning Theological Education," 12.
17. Adapted from Cronshaw, 13.

These six models also highlight the variety of theological education that is available today. There is theological training for laity, for training in ministerial theology, in professional theology and in academic theology. Each requires a different curriculum and has different goals. Theological institutions need to be clear as to what they hope to accomplish as this will determine the model of theological training that they use.

Connecting Curriculum to Context

While different models of theological education are a result of specific needs of the church at a point of time in history or in a specific location, how does a theological institution today intentionally connect with its context? How does one connect curriculum with context so that the graduates are effective?

The basic principle is that education is for a purpose. So a theological institution does not exist to produce graduates, but to meet needs in churches, the mission field and in Christian organizations. It does so through its graduates. The effectiveness of a theological institution is then assessed not by how many graduates it has produced and the quality of the graduates, but whether the graduates have been able to meet the needs of churches, mission agencies and the communities where they work. Was its curriculum relevant to the context of the graduates?

This principle of "education for a purpose" is illustrated through what is referred to as a program logic. What this means is that an activity produces a result. There is a cause-and-effect relationship. In education, this means that teaching results in learning. We then assess whether learning has taken place through exams, research and reflection papers, case studies, simulations, field practice and a variety of other assessment tools.

There is a difference between a training activity and the result of the activity. The objective is not to report how many attended the training activity but what changed as a result of the activity. I think most seminaries understand this well and are able to assess whether learning has taken place.

However, the assessment of the training activity does not end with determining whether learning took place. If education is for a purpose, then what did the graduate do with what he or she learnt?

Theological institutions, like any other educational institution, exist within a context. There are two models of organizational theory. One is a systems theory of organizations. An organization has a structure, clearly defined roles, processes and procedures, a product (in this case, a curriculum), and so on. The more clearly these are defined, the more effective the organization is. So the quality of the institution is measured by its systems and procedures, and by the resources it has in terms of curriculum, faculty, facilities, library, and so on. You will hear terms like ISO 9000. A lot of our accreditation is based on this theory of organizations. While context is sometimes acknowledged, a systems theory of organizations is mostly internally focused.

Others see an organization as a living system – an organism. They move away from a mechanistic model of an institution to a more biological model. An organization is an open system. It has a structure, but it survives and is able to thrive if it is able to adapt to changes in its context and environment. The open systems approach requires organizational structure, systems and procedures to be flexible, responsive and adaptable. Such organizations are sensitive to context and are externally focused.

Both understandings of organizations are needed for the quality and effectiveness of a theological institution. There is a need for both an internal focus and an external focus.

Pulling these ideas together, we get what is referred to as a program logic for a theological institution.

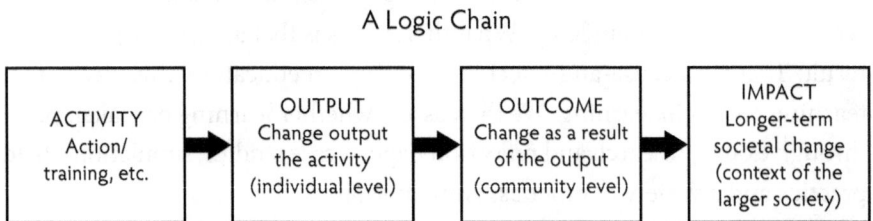

A Logic Chain

ACTIVITY Action/ training, etc.	OUTPUT Change output the activity (individual level)	OUTCOME Change as a result of the output (community level)	IMPACT Longer-term societal change (context of the larger society)

Figure 3: Program Logic

An *Activity* – training provided by a seminary – results in changes in an individual. These changes are referred to as the *Output*.

This changed individual – the graduate – is then able to effectively minister in a church, a mission field or a Christian organization. The effectiveness of the graduate and the changes that occur in the church or the mission field as a result are called the *Outcome*. Note that this is different from what we often refer to as educational outcomes.

Finally, the local church or the community of believers has an influence on the surrounding community, and this is referred to as the *Impact*.

There is a cause-and-effect relationship from the activity all the way to impact. A lot of other factors that can affect and disrupt the cause-and-effect process need to be taken into account. These external and internal factors are known as risks and are identified and addressed if and when possible.

There are a number of implications of this:

a) The focus of the theological institution needs to be at the *Outcome* level and not on the *Output*. The graduate and his or her training is only a means to an end.

b) The theological institution's effectiveness is measured by the effectiveness of its graduates in the contexts where they minister.

c) This means that the context of the graduates needs to be understood and as a result needs to influence the curriculum of the theological institution.

So how does one then connect the context of the graduates with the curriculum of the theological institution?

To be able to connect curriculum with context, two organizational processes are critical in order to ensure the effectiveness of the seminary. The first is that there need to be administrative mechanisms that ensure feedback is collected at various points in the process. The second is that there need to be clear administrative mechanisms for decisions to be made based on the feedback and information that has been gathered.

a) *Feedback Mechanisms:* An educational institution needs to have feedback mechanisms to assess the progress and quality of the programs. An exam, for example, assesses the progress of the student. A student evaluation of a course provides some information about the effectiveness of the faculty. A monthly financial report provides a snapshot in time of the financial status of the organization. So there need to be mechanisms at the activity, output and outcome levels that gather information and provide feedback on progress and changes taking place. While most institutions have internal feedback mechanisms, very few have mechanisms to get feedback from their external context on a regular basis.

b) *Decision-Making:* Good decisions are made on the basis of accurate information and feedback from various parts of the organization. It is not uncommon for information to be gathered and then not used. For example, when a curriculum revision is being done, are the student and faculty evaluations of the courses looked at? Is feedback obtained from graduates and the churches and mission agencies where they are working? Feedback from assessments, student and faculty evaluations, and student performance needs to be directed to specific educational administrators who have the ability to make the decisions regarding redesign of the curriculum or revision of specific courses. Too often, evaluations are done, but the information is never used to make the educational program more relevant.

Figure 4 shows how a feedback mechanism for a seminary could look.

A number of key points about feedback mechanisms from the diagram:

- As each Activity/course is conducted and then completed, the effectiveness of the Activity needs to be assessed. This is done through faculty assessments of the courses, student assessments of the curriculum and student evaluations of the faculty.
- The seminary's main function is to train and equip leaders. The Output, then, is that leaders are properly and adequately equipped. This is the easiest level of assessment. Most seminaries have already established Graduate Profiles or Graduation Requirements for every program that they run. Throughout their time at a seminary, students are continually being assessed as to whether they are in the process of fulfilling the Graduation Requirements. This is done through tests, exams, assignments, projects, case studies, and so on. The changes in the student's knowledge, attitudes and behaviour/skills are what is being assessed.
- Any seminary's mission should never be to only equip leaders. Equipped leaders need to serve. A seminary's mission should be to serve the church and mission agencies involved in the Great Commission and the Great Commandment, and it does that by

equipping leaders. Measuring the Outcome, therefore, is done by assessing whether the churches and mission organizations are being served by the graduates. The right tools are needed to answer this question and the assessment needs to be done by working closely with the churches and ministry contexts where the graduates are serving.

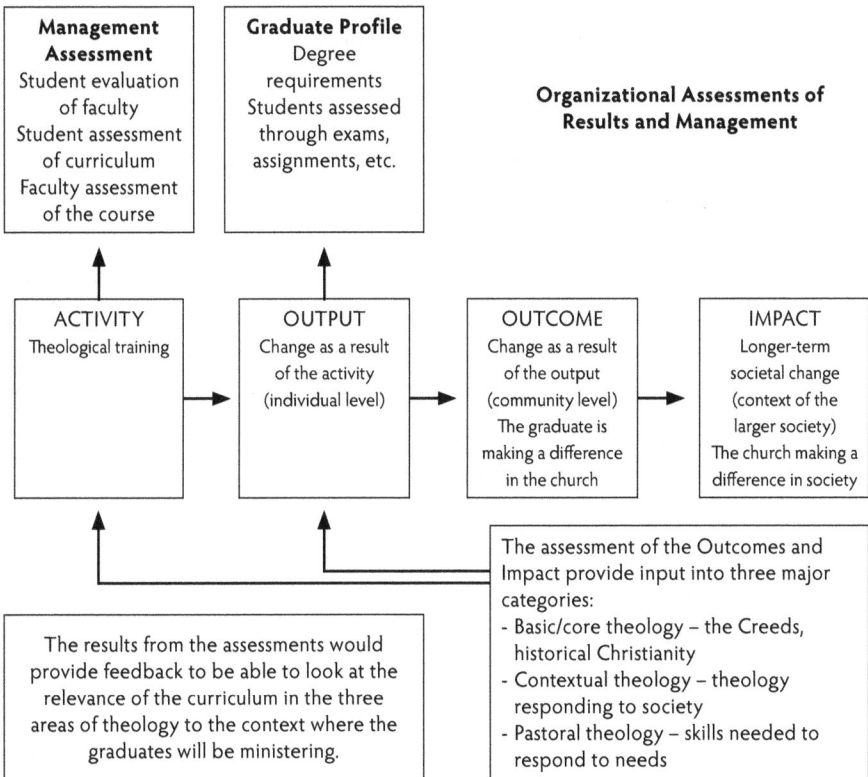

Management Assessment	Graduate Profile		
Student evaluation of faculty Student assessment of curriculum Faculty assessment of the course	Degree requirements Students assessed through exams, assignments, etc.	Organizational Assessments of Results and Management	
ACTIVITY	**OUTPUT**	**OUTCOME**	**IMPACT**
Theological training	Change as a result of the activity (individual level)	Change as a result of the output (community level) The graduate is making a difference in the church	Longer-term societal change (context of the larger society) The church making a difference in society
		The assessment of the Outcomes and Impact provide input into three major categories: - Basic/core theology – the Creeds, historical Christianity - Contextual theology – theology responding to society - Pastoral theology – skills needed to respond to needs	
The results from the assessments would provide feedback to be able to look at the relevance of the curriculum in the three areas of theology to the context where the graduates will be ministering.			

Figure 4: Organizational Assessments and Feedback Loops

- At the Outcome level, periodic assessments of ministry contexts of the graduates (churches and/or communities) would provide a wealth of information for the redesign of the curriculum or revision of specific courses. Feedback from the graduates, the church community and key Christian leaders, as well as the community, will provide information for the revision of the three aspects of theological education:

a) *Basic/Core Theological Truths:* These would include the Creeds, Systematic or Biblical Theology, and Historical Theology. While all theological concepts are important for any theological education, are specific theological concepts problematic in particular contexts? Students need not only to know what these are, but also to understand how to address them.

b) *Contextual Theology:* How is God perceived and understood in a particular context or culture? The issue of Christian ethics in various contexts is critical. What are biblical perspectives on the issues of poverty and social justice, gender, race, human trafficking, immigrants, female genital mutilation, and so on? What are the specific social and ethical issues in a particular context that need to be addressed from within a Christian ethical framework? How is respect shown, and thus God worshipped, in a specific culture and context?

c) *Pastoral Theology:* Are individuals and families struggling with specific issues that a graduate would know how to address? There are cultural variations on issues such as child-raising and child discipline, husband–wife relationships and divorce, issues with in-laws in extended family situations, gender roles, selection of marriage partners, and so on. Pastoral issues may also encompass problems related with recent converts, such as persecution, baptism, being cut off from the family and community, polygamy, and so on.

These feedback loops then connect curriculum to the context of the theological institution and to that of the graduates. Connecting curriculum to context increases the probability of the graduates being effective in the churches and mission fields they minister in.

A program logic – such as going from the activity of theological training, to ensuring that the output is as per the graduate profile, to thus ensuring the outcome of enabling the graduates to be effective in their ministry contexts – is the model that begins to ensure that theological education can have an impact.

Conclusion

To conclude: if all ministry, as Eugene Peterson says, is geographical – meaning located geographically in a specific cultural, political and historical reality – do theological institutions understand the realities and contexts of graduates and prepare them accordingly? Do they intentionally connect their curricula to their contexts?

Some of you may be thinking that this is basic educational theory, and after all, isn't this the way much of education should be? American writer and philosopher Walker Percy, in describing his art, writes, " . . . you are telling the reader or listener or the viewer something he already knows but which he doesn't quite know that he knows, so that in the act of communication he experiences a recognition, a feeling that he has been there before, a shock of recognition."[18] My prayer is that there have been some "Aha!" moments – moments of recognition – for you.

To end, I would like to go back to the life of Polycarp. We have talked much about the effectiveness of graduates in the contexts where they minister. In the life of Polycarp there is another quality that the apostle John ensured was built into his disciple: that of faithfulness in the midst of the context.

While Polycarp was effective in safeguarding the faith by countering the heresies of Marcion, when confronted by the theology of the Roman Empire and its worship of Caesar, there was no way to counter it other than to remain

---

18. Walker Percy, in Lewis A. Lawson and Victor A. Kramer, eds., *Conversations with Walker Percy* (Jackson, MS: University Press of Mississippi, 1985), 24.

faithful. Polycarp was martyred because he would not proclaim that Caesar was lord. As he faced execution by burning, he declared, "86 years have I served him, and he has done me no wrong. How can I blaspheme my King and my Saviour?"

Effectiveness and faithfulness – the two indicators that show that curriculum is connected to context.

Discussion Questions

1. The starting point for discussing curriculum is "What is the purpose of our institution/organization and its programs of study?" How would you answer this question? Describe one or two ways in which your institution/organization might build a stronger shared understanding of its purpose.

2. Quality education promotes ongoing processes of management assessment through such means as student evaluation of courses and faculty, faculty assessments of the organization and administration, and assessment of the faculty conducted by the President or Dean. Describe some of the practices done in your institution/organization. Give at least one suggestion for how these processes might be strengthened.

3. A missional purpose for theological education sees as the final goal meaningful impact on society through the ministry of the church. Stakeholder feedback on both successes and challenges in societal impact then becomes a key means for instructing the curriculum.

- In what ways does your institution/organization seek feedback from alumni (output) and the churches they serve (outcome)? To what extent is the focus primarily backwards (assessment of the curriculum as it has been) or forwards (current societal trends and challenges and implications for the future shape of the curriculum)?
- There are many potential barriers to gaining meaningful feedback from community leaders (impact), especially when these have little or no sympathy for local churches. Describe one or two possible strategies whereby your institution/organization might access and benefit from the observations and insights of community leaders.

- The final step in connecting curriculum and context is allowing feedback to instruct curricular change. What (if any) are the processes whereby your institution/organization institutes meaningful stakeholder-informed curricular change? Give one or two suggestions how this process might be strengthened.

4

My Assessment Journey

Ashish Chrispal

Regional Director, Asia, Overseas Council India

Assessing students to see their progress is not new to Asia. Examination is built into the Asian culture of education. I still remember when my yet-to-be-three-year-old had to appear for his admission to pre-nursery for an interview with three teachers in three different sections of a hall. Each child was asked to recite a nursery rhyme, to write the letters of the alphabet as the teacher directed and to write the numbers from one to one hundred, again, as the teacher required. As my son began pre-school it was marked by a daily quiz, a weekly test, a unit test, a monthly test and term exam, a mid-year exam and the final exam. Even though the Indian Government has banned entrance exams for children, the exam culture continues to be used to evaluate learning throughout the rest of the educational journey. I feel this creates a negative attitude towards assessment across the educational world.

I have been involved in theological education for the last forty-five years, first as a student, but mainly as a facilitator. I am used to seeing seminaries advertise their achievements in terms of numbers of graduates going into pastoral ministry, serving as missionaries or involved in some kind of Christian service. I have come to realize that this is purely output data which never gives us the real picture as to our fulfilment of our mission and vision. To put it differently, are we doing what we say we are doing? My journey to look at educational assessment began with my seven years with an international school. The need for assessment of our theological institutional mission, vision and goals came home to me as I was invited by Overseas Council Australia and the Arab Baptist Theological Seminary, Beirut, to be part of the Assessment Project in 2012. I have been thrilled to learn how assessment of our seminaries can help us to be faithful, in the true sense of our calling as described by Paul in Ephesians 4:7–16. Are we equipping the body of Christ to grow in Christ towards maturity, which includes our privilege to be disciples and disciplers of the nations? Are we the agents of transformation, helping our graduates to be transformed and be those agents in society? Here, in this short essay, I want to share some of the key learning outcomes for me as I was involved with three schools in their journey of assessing their programs. The ultimate goal is to redesign our curriculum in the light of our research into the process of assessment.

Five Key Areas of Assessment Impact for the Seminary

First, assessment is necessary to make a difference in who we are and what we intend as our outcomes. However, beyond outputs and outcomes is the vast area of impact in society. The question that continues to be asked, particularly of us as theological educators, is: How far are our alumni impacting the church and, through the church, the surrounding community and society in general?

Second, it helped me to understand the impact that assessment has on our implicit and explicit curriculums. It also leads to create "a culture of assessment," which in turn helps us to redesign our curriculum and sharpen our mission and vision as the generations keep on changing.

Third, the process of assessment enhances our endeavour in the holistic development of students beyond head knowledge and mere cerebral growth. The involvement of head, heart and hands in the ministry becomes vital as we involve our alumni in the assessment and listen to their needs for being effective in their ministry to the world.

Fourth, assessment provides unparalleled research opportunities in discovering how adults learn and, in particular, how they learn values and perspectives, and the information needed to develop these skills. It further enhances our understanding of how they train habits of mind that characterize our respective fields.

Fifth, assessment benefits us by building meaning into the broader processes of program and institutional assessment. Many theological educational institutions want to be trendy and want to either comply with the requirements of the accreditation agencies or justify their programs through the assessment process. Others are tempted to obstruct assessment for fear of its negative impact on the publicity of the institution. Some want to minimize the assessment process as an imitation of the management world and thus undermine its value. But the reality is that we assess our students continually to benefit their learning. In similar vein, assessment of the institution benefits our own endeavour to impact and equip the body of Christ.

My own learning reiterated for me the purpose of theological education to be missional and thus to be rooted in the Word of God and engaged with the world that God has created. This in turn will enhance our alumni and the church we serve to be agents of God's mission. Assessment challenges us to wrestle with the reality of our goals accomplished through our alumni and the purpose for which we exist.

Seven Essential Qualities of Institutional Assessment

It is crucial that we see assessment as a means and not as an end in itself. Assessment of the program or institution is not merely for gathering data. Our goals and values must be defined by the information/data we gather.

Second, assessment must help us to achieve educational benefits along with establishing our accountability. We must allow the assessment process and culture to improve our students' learning processes, as well as increase our knowledge about the processes.

Third, our context must guide our assessment purposes, goals and methods. We need to seek the kind of information that will make a positive difference to our endeavour. This also helps us to recognize that theological education has both universal essentials and contextual dimensions in providing relevant education.

Fourth, fruitful assessment information enhances and encourages comparison of diverse programs. The multiplicity of the results guides the very uniqueness of the institution. Today, in many Asian nations theological education has become a business, and most of the curricula are stereotypes. The assessment process helps to bring a unique dimension to each institution that makes a difference, through its alumni, to its communities and nation.

Fifth, assessment enhances the coherence within our programs. Since the assessment process draws on multiple modes of inquiry, it helps us to re-examine our explicit and implicit educational goals and student outcomes.

Sixth, we need critically communicated information or feedback for a successful assessment. The Asian worldview suffers from a higher culture context, in which honest feedback from alumni about faculty, leadership and governance of the alma mata is difficult to obtain. However, assessment needs honest and frank feedback to be a positive influence for an effective future of the institution and its program.

Finally, assessment can yield better results when done in the spirit of the transformative goal. However, it can be detrimental if it is done for mere compliance or justification of institutional existence.

Constructing Assessment Context

As theological institutions, we are called by God to make a lasting impact upon the lives of people. This means we need a long-term commitment to a dynamic plan for our institution, and thus a commitment to a culture of assessment that is transformative. This provides stability, relevance and tools to deal with the complexity of our strategic planning. And this in turn helps us to create an atmosphere of purpose.

We need to rely on faculty questions for direction. The faculty must buy into the process, as assessment results help faculty to plan and function better. There needs to be a direct correlation between the subject goals (objectives) and the mission and vision of the institution. The assessment data provides a direct loop to enable the faculty to recognize the purpose of the program and its role in the institution.

Educators are able to discern the validity and relevance of tools, and recognize the credible interpretations of results. Maintaining the involvement of the faculty in developing instruments of assessment brings credibility to the process. The process becomes effective only through the interaction of the faculty. The interactive nature of assessment enhances alumni and student involvement in program assessment.

There is a greater need for defining the criteria and comparison publicly. Making public the assessment criteria evolved by the faculty brings consensus on goals, standards and criteria among the stakeholders. It gives a much-needed transparency to the institution, especially in the context where there is a great divide between the church and the seminaries.

This in turn leads to the need to translate results into relevant "live" information. In reality, effectively transmitted assessment information often raises more questions than it provides answers. Therefore, the data needs to be made understandable. The assessment process must help faculty know the learning process for educational goals, the motivations of students, and their personal growth, abilities and learning styles.

Finally, the data gathered must lead to change. It must move us as institutions from data to decisions. We must work on creative feedback that can stimulate improvement. The process of assessment must touch the very core of our existence and curriculum to help us be more effective in our vision and mission of equipping God's people to be fruitful in being witnesses in the world, and thus be obedient to Jesus Christ's Great Commission.

In conclusion, let me say that we, as theological institutions, under the Lord and his church, have the great responsibility of preparing agents of transformation for God's mission in the world. The assessment process will help us and will enhance our ministry to be effective and impactful as we interact with people at various levels within and outside the church.

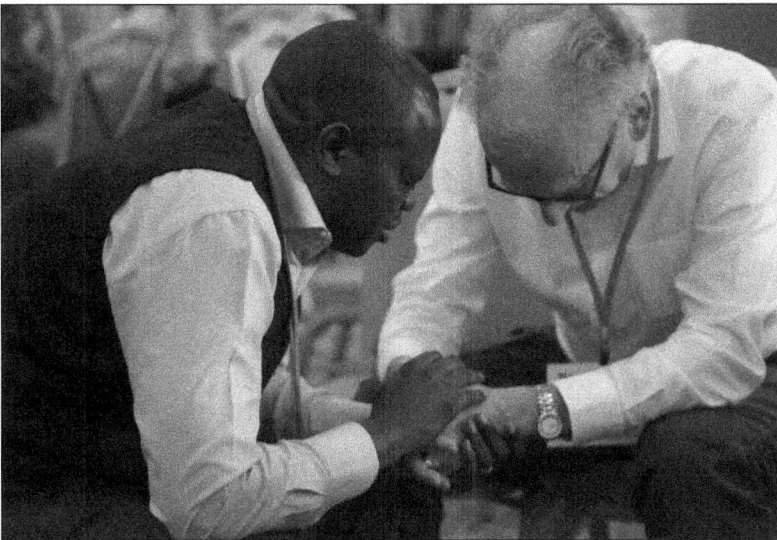

Discussion Questions

1. What do you think Ashish means when he talks about building "a culture of assessment" which shapes both the implicit and explicit curricula? Describe one or two actions your organization might take to better promote a culture of assessment.

2. Most educational institutions place their primary evaluative emphases on the assessment of head knowledge and cerebral growth, and yet Ashish sees the holistic "involvement of head, heart and hands" as crucial to effective ministry formation. How do your current assessment processes seek to evaluate each of head (cognitive), heart (affective) and hands (behavioural)? Suggest one or two ways in which assessment for holistic formation could be better promoted and implemented.

3. "We must allow the assessment process and culture to improve our students' learning processes, as well as increase our knowledge about the processes." Describe one or two ways in which meaningful assessment might impact not merely the overall curricular structure, but the quality of classroom instruction, with the end result of stronger holistic learning.

4. "Today, in many Asian nations theological education has become a business, and most of the curricula are stereotypes." To what extent would you see this negative portrayal as descriptive of your curriculum? In what ways have you sought to innovate such that your curriculum better serves the mission of the church in its context?

5. Meaningful change can only be implemented with faculty "buy-in." What are some key steps by which your institution/organization might promote faculty ownership of the assessment process and resulting curricular change?

Section II

Stories from the Field

Institutions Which Assessed Their Context and Changed Their Curriculum

We turn now from the more theoretical issues of researching context in order to redesign curricula to four practical examples of how this was done. These case studies are selected from among the ten seminaries which presented at the ICETE 2015 Triennial.

Each of the ten had been "heading in this direction" in various ways for a year or two prior to being selected for the intensive work of 2014 and 2015. Nonetheless, all these schools found that there was much work to be done to achieve the goals in under two years so that they would be ready to present in Antalya. They had to determine the scope of what they wanted to do; work with stakeholders; design their research and conduct it; run curriculum workshops; and decide what changes to make.

As you will read, these four institutions have completed the task up to a certain stage. None has been able to re-examine the changes after implementation. However, one key to the strategy is that the changes they made are based on research they did. These curricula changes are not driven by a theory, so much as the theory is driven by the results of their research. This is a key concept because it allows for an objectivity in decision-making. It brings the imperative for change clearly into view, and gives impetus to the change process.

You will notice that each case study in this section ends up in a very different place. Each implements different changes from the others. They all devise their new curricula in different directions. The Indian example leads to a deepening of the non-academic elements of their program. The Sri Lankan example leads to understanding the subtleties of staff members' behaviour and to "letting go some staff"! The Colombian example helped the curriculum redesign to truly address the major issue of displaced people and their needs in the country. The Zimbabwean example ended up with a complete re-imagining of the curriculum to help students move from an African worldview to a biblical one, all the while embedding in the African context.

This variety of changes is exactly what is expected and needed. No two seminaries have the same context or calling from God. Thus each one can expect some difference from the others, as each undertakes research and determines how to be responsive to particular contexts and callings.

Through the questions at the end of each chapter you are invited to consider your context and the processes you might explore on your journey to a new, more relevant curriculum.

5

A Colombian Experience:

Doing Research in the
Context of Displacement

Jhohan Centeno
Faculty member, Fundación Universitaria Seminario Bíblico de Colombia

The evangelical church in Colombia is a diverse church that serves in different social contexts and in different realities. One of the realities with which the church is faced is displacement. "Without a doubt, forced displacement is a very violent social and subjective experience, and sadly it is part of the historical configuration of the memory of citizens of Colombia."[1] Amid this harsh socio-political reality, the educational institution Fundación Universitaria Seminario Bíblico de Colombia (FUSBC) combines the development of its research work with the realities of this context, taking into account institutional and ecclesiastical factors. On the one hand, there is a need to contribute to building the social fabric in order to fulfil one element of the institutional mission. On the other hand, there is the imperative to offer students a better understanding of the problems of the country as an alternative component of ministry training that contributes to more relevant ecclesiastical work within the Colombian contextual reality. Additionally there is the reality that Pentecostal churches represent a majority in the Colombian ecclesiastical scenario.

---

1. J. D. Demera, "Ciudad, migración y religión: Etnografía de los recursos identitarios y de la religiosidad de los desplazados en altos de Cazucá," *Theologica Xaveriana* (2007): 304.

Within this framework, the FUSBC Instructor-Directed Student Research Group (IDSRG) of Pentecostalism was created as a means of studying the reality of churches with a Pentecostal background. Since 2012, the IDSRG has been investigating the Colombian Pentecostal church. Using bibliographical research and field studies, it has sought to understand the reality of the so-called "Pentecostal phenomenon." In 2014, the IDSRG investigated the work of Pentecostals among the population that has suffered forced displacement due to violence in the country. This approach had a dual purpose: first, to increase the visibility of the social action of Pentecostal churches in the country; and, second, to respond to academic approaches that assert that Pentecostalism is in denial of the present reality.[2] The present investigative response is built on an interdenominational foundation, but with Pentecostal participation.

Undertaking the study of the Pentecostal phenomenon required an open methodological approach, one that follows patterns common to sociology and the study of population groups. It began with a review of the literature on Pentecostalism in Colombia. This was followed in turn by the study of some approaches to Chilean Pentecostalism, which, besides having experienced an unusual rise, has been widely investigated. Once the theoretical basis was established, development proceeded in parallel with various research methodologies. Quantitative research was performed on various congregations in Medellín and in the Aburrá Valley. In addition, surveys were conducted of leaders of churches classified as traditional Pentecostal churches.[3] Students with different regional and church backgrounds developed participant observations in the churches studied. Combining data with the collection of this information has resulted in a better understanding of the Pentecostal phenomenon on the part of IDSRG participants.

From this investigative work, some initial conclusions have emerged about the theology, liturgy and social work of the Pentecostal churches in Colombia. When considering the scope of the social work of these churches, it must

---

2. This approach has its basis in Spanish, mainly in the book *El refugio de las masas* (*The Refuge of the Masses*) by Lalive d'Epinay, which is followed by quite a few authors writing about the evangelical church in Latin America.

3. The definition of "traditional Pentecostal" is made along theological and not liturgical lines. These theological lines followed Donald W. Dayton, *Theological Roots of Pentecostalism* (Peabody, MA: Hendrickson, 2000).

be understood that Pentecostal theological work is not given as a written doctrinal formulation, but rather as a practice that is usually liturgical. To the greatest extent, it is in the context of the worship service that the social work of Pentecostal churches to the displaced population in this country is begun. Colombian Pentecostal churches are embedded in all sectors of society, but they are especially prevalent in marginalized sectors at the periphery where they experience significant growth, not in the form of mega-churches, but in the proliferation of small groups. We found some authors affirming that "in Pentecostal churches, the faithful find new communities of social support, new family structures and values, and they also learn a new self-discipline and confidence in God, all of which encourages them to move forward and to adapt themselves to an insecure and inconsistent labor market."[4] This is highly relevant for ministerial understanding and practice, especially because "a person displaced by violence in Colombia, instead of sending God out of his life because of all the suffering he has had to endure, welcomes Him all the more and recognizes more vividly the power of the Divine in his life."[5]

Researching the social work of the Pentecostal church has led IDSRG participants to seek understanding about other facets of the Pentecostal church, such as its liturgical work, its theological teaching and its integration in social spaces. Investigating and learning from a church that serves amid adverse circumstances will contribute to the comprehensive training offered by an institution that is convinced of the need to serve God, the church and society as part of its mission.

Discussion Questions

FUSBC has sought to make connection between curriculum and context through a specialized Instructor-Directed Student Research Group (IDSRG), focusing on the patterns of community life evident in the Colombian Pentecostal church.

---

4. M. Lindhardt, "La Globalización Pentecostal: Difusión, Apropiación y Orientación Global," *Cultura & Religión* (2011): 119.
5. N. Mafla, "Función de la religión en la vida de las víctimas del desplazamiento forzado en Colombia" (PhD diss., Universidad Complutense de Madrid, 2012), 161.

1. If your institution/organization was to undertake significant field research in your context, what might be one or two of the most pressing issues that you believe should be researched? Why do you believe that these issues are so important?

2. FUSBC sees as imperative a cooperative effort between faculty and students in the development of contextual research. If you were to develop a comparable research team, who among your faculty might be key players in leading such a team? How might you involve your students meaningfully in this sort of research?

6

An Indian Experience:
Seeing the Gaps

Havilah Dharamraj
Dean of Academics, South Asian Institute of Advanced Christian Studies, India

SAIACS conducted a Research-Driven Curriculum Revision (RDCR) of its flagship program, the MTh (Master of Theology). We surveyed a sample of alumni from the year 2000 onwards using online surveys and focus-group discussions. We developed questionnaires separately for the different target groups, namely, alumni and their ministry placements. In the latter category we had separate questionnaires for employers, peers and employees.

Once the survey results began to come in, the trickle soon turned into an avalanche. Our defence against getting buried under was to grab a set of five fluorescent highlighter pens. With these we identified the major trends.

First, let me outline the process we followed, and then the way we analyzed the results. From the data, we isolated five trends which focused out attention on our strengths and areas for improvement. Here is part of the story.

Process
Step 1: Collation of Data from Online Survey and Focus Groups

- Timeframe: one month
- Personnel: Academic Office Administrator, one collator for online material, two transcribers

Step 2: Identification of Significant Trends

- Timeframe: one month
- Personnel: Principal, Academic Dean, Student Dean

Significant trends identified by questions which elicited the most comments.

Trends

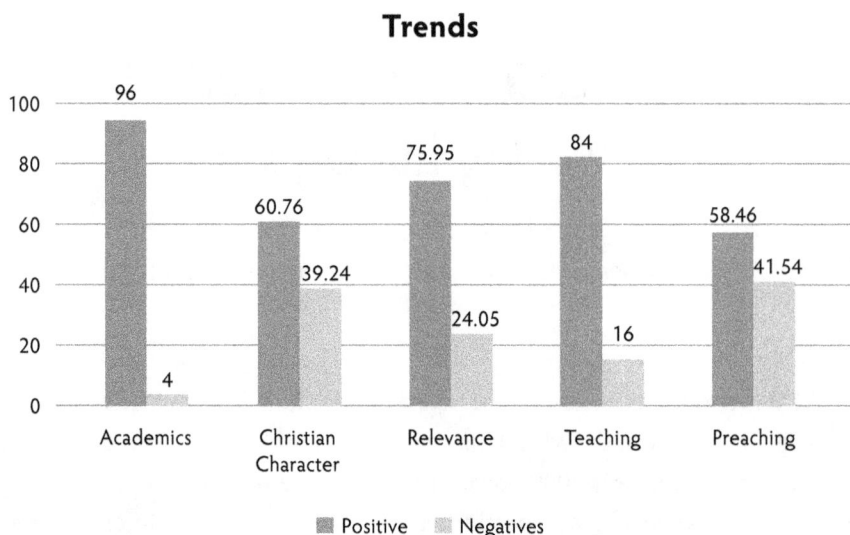

The responses to the academic content of the college program revealed a higher proportional sense of satisfaction with the overall curriculum, as revealed in the following analysis.

Step 3: Studying the Trend

- Timeframe: one month
- Personnel: Academic Office Administrator, Principal, Academic Dean, Student Dean

Step 4: Action

The action relevant to each trend is shown after discussion of each trend.

Trend 1: Academics

Comments included:

- the kind of academic fervour found in SAIACS graduates is praiseworthy
- confident in their subject matter
- have evangelical convictions
- have the aptitude to excel at higher education
- grateful that several of our faculty have SAIACS degrees
- SAIACS's contribution to evangelical theological education is unparalleled
- A SAIACS alumnus helped us revise our curriculum and syllabus . . . he explained mission statement, objectives . . .

Picking out the major elements in the trend:
SAIACS is serving the church well through academics. Specifically:

- independent research
- critical thinking/analytical skills
- intellectual objectivity
- subject expertise
- strategic thinking

The inference drawn from this is that this part of the college life is consistently good, hence:

Action: Way to go! Keep at it!

Trend 2: Christian Formation

Comments included:

Doing well . . .

- gladly undertakes menial tasks like cleaning the bathroom, but not for the approval of others
- has a good relationship with staff and students . . . very good team player
- is humble . . . available to do anything
- works diligently
- goes the extra mile to assist students and colleagues in need
- is honest, sincere and committed. We believe that these character traits were nurtured by SAIACS
- encourages others
- spent several nights in the hospital tending a student with jaundice

- open to advice from leaders
- works hard for no financial gain

Once in a while we hear students say that because of the academic rigour the temptation is to put spiritual formation on the backburner. We found that this could be true in a few of our graduates.

Can do better . . .

- had a good beginning but could not end well
- tends to be comfort-seeking after being at a comfortable place like SAIACS
- knows what he should do but does not follow through
- rigid . . . needs to be flexible

Picking out the major elements in the trend:

What SAICS is doing well:

- Living in an egalitarian ethos – 18%
- Cell groups/fellowship dinners – 24%
- Eco-friendly campus – 15%
- Sharing and caring community – 15%

What SAIACS can do better:

- Intentional assistance with spiritual growth
- Personal counselling/mentoring
- Intentionally integrate the academic and spiritual

These mixed results led to the inference that remedial action is needed in this area. As it happened, we had taken cognisance of this trend even before this survey, and some remedial action had already begun. Our survey results affirmed that we had taken steps in the right direction.

Remedial Action: SAIACS needed to increase its emphasis on Christian formation.

To this end a Retreat-in-Daily-Life program was introduced as well as a system of personal mentoring within cell groups.

Trend 3: Relevance to Ministry in South Asia

Including leadership skills and mission-centred thinking.

Employers, peers, employees said . . .	SAIACS graduates said . . .
SAIACS graduates are effective missionaries.	I would have liked more exposure to mission agencies when at SAIACS.
Please teach your students the contemporary challenges to missions.	SAIACS developed in me a passion to make the gospel relevant and contextual.
This SAIACS graduate is a great visionary in the mission field.	I would have liked a firsthand experience of cross-cultural missions by travelling to mission fields.
SAIACS needs to balance academics with real-life issues.	I wish I had learned church and office management.
SAIACS deals excellently with scholarly issues, correlating classroom learning with issues faced in a local ministry setting.	I would have liked to study more on current ethical issues.
SAIACS graduates can be readily entrusted with new initiatives.	I would have appreciated help with correlating classroom learning with issues faced in a local ministry setting.
SAIACS graduates need to develop a concern for justice issues.	I wish I had studied moral issues.
SAIACS grads are creative in teaching, are able to understand the context and rightly adapt the subject to the audience.	
SAIACS must develop the competency to integrate across disciplines for the advancement of mission.	
SAIACS alumni don't understand the culture of the local neighbourhood.	
SAIACS students perform really well even in stressful situations.	
SAIACS graduates have excellent leadership abilities.	

Picking out the major elements in the trend:

What SAIACS is doing well:

- Inculcating a zeal for missions
- Developing leadership abilities

What SAIACS can do better:

- Provide exposure in mission work
- Integrate academics with contemporary issues

Inference: more negative than positive results; remedial action needed

Action: Trend 3 was a mixed bag. With our motto of "Excellence for Mission," this trend looked at the effectiveness of our alumni in the mission field . . .

- SAIACS could better integrate academics and the South Asian context.
- As a result of these findings a Context Based Learning course at MA level was introduced as well as the increasing use of field experts as Missions faculty.
- At MTh level, there is a need to intentionally address application to contextual and contemporary issues.

Trends 4 and 5 were dealt with in a similar way.

Summary of Findings

One by one, we systematically identified, studied and talked over the five trends we isolated from the avalanche of feedback. Here is the summary of our findings and of the action initiated in response to those findings.

Looking back, we think the RDCR was one of the most interesting exercises we've undertaken – and certainly a fruitful one. We would unhesitatingly recommend it for the health of any theological institution.

- *Trend 1.* In academics SAIACS is serving the church well.
- *Trend 2.* In the creation of Christian character, SAIACS needs to increase its emphasis in this area.
- *Trend 3.* In its relevance to ministry in South Asia, SAIACS could better integrate academics with the South Asian context.
- *Trend 4.* In teaching, SAIACS could train students in teaching.
- *Trend 5.* More needs to be done in the area of training students in the art of preaching.

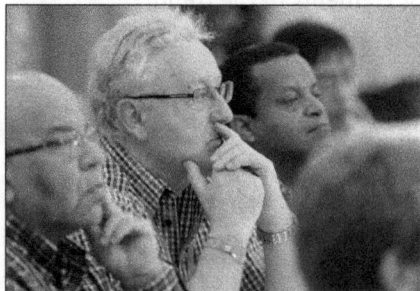

Discussion Questions

The report from SAIACS documents a four-step process for translating research into action: (1) collation of data; (2) identification of significant trends; (3) studying the trends; (4) action.

1. For this process to be effective there needs to be a clear understanding of who will be responsible at each stage. For your school, who do you think might be most appropriate to take leadership and/or be involved in facilitating each of the four suggested stages of movement from research to action?

2. In that the faculty ultimately need to implement curricular change, what are some key ways you can ensure that your faculty have "ownership" of change?

3. What do you anticipate might be some of the main barriers to effective engagement with any or all of the four suggested steps? Suggest one or two ways in which these barriers might be overcome.

7

A Zimbabwean Experience:
Journey to Maturity

Ray Motsi, President, and Robert Heaton, Academic Dean
Theological College of Zimbabwe

We are on the top of the mountain and there is an ambivalent feeling about it. On the one hand, we are so excited that we have been able to achieve this, yet on the other hand, there is some kind of apprehension about the future.

Background

It all started with the conference in Beirut where we were introduced to Arab Baptist Theological Seminary (ABTS) which had recently completed this mammoth and unbelievable task of devising their own curriculum which was flexible and contextual. We wondered whether some of us who had always used the classical missionary-initiated curriculum would really be able to walk away without any sense of betrayal and loss of loyalty to those founding and faithful fathers. We were assured of some help from those who were connected to the missionaries and had travelled longer on that journey. Dr Perry Shaw, who had led the process at ABTS, was more than willing to come to Zimbabwe and he started us off on this long and meandering journey. Dr John Jusu from OCI (Overseas Council International) also visited us and was on standby and available for our convenience if we needed him to encourage those of us who were hesitant and afraid of the unknown.

OCI, with their generous support as usual, dangled a carrot by offering some sponsorship to help us in the process.

When we got back home, the first thing was to devise a Gantt chart which would show a clear path of where we were going, how we were going to get there, the various important steps, the timeline and the tools we needed to do it. We then conferred with Dr Shaw and Dr Jusu as to when they would visit us in Zimbabwe. Once this was arranged, there was no turning back; we had burnt our bridges, as it were.

Ownership and Responsibility

Whereas Dr Robert Heaton, as Academic Dean, was the nerve-link driving the process as the person to whom the interviewers and faculty were reporting, Dr Ray Motsi had oversight of the whole project as the head of the institution in terms of communicating with the board, sourcing the funding and guiding the vision of where we wanted to go. Communication was critical as everybody had to know who was in charge of which tasks, and where to go if they had questions. We also made sure that everybody knew that we were all responsible since this was a Theological College of Zimbabwe project.

Territorial Battles

On the home front, we had been asked by the board to write a new curriculum. The problem was that we had always used the cut-and-paste principle on the good old missionary-initiated classic curriculum. We ended up with about fifty-six modules for the whole BA Theology program. The students were not coping with the workload. Even though this was too much, there was very little we could do to change it since the departmental territorial battle lines were always drawn every time we started talking of reducing the curriculum. Crucially, then, the research-driven revision was an opportunity and a window for us to do this important process from an objective point of view. TCZ was started in 1979 by Africa Evangelical Fellowship (AEF), now SIM (Servants In Mission), and, apart from some contextualization of courses, we had not changed the curriculum framework in any major way. Yet our context had changed markedly since Independence in 1980. Hence the revision project was long overdue.

We started by calling a meeting with all the faculty to explain the challenge from Beirut, what we had decided to do and how we were going to do it. Thank God that the majority of the faculty were open and willing to come on board, but obviously there were a few who were not sure why we should change.

Market Survey

A decision was made to select six groups of people from among TCZ stakeholders whom we would target for interviews. These were alumni (pastors), alumni (para-church), non-TCZ pastors/leaders, churches with social ministries, current students and Christian business people. Questionnaires were designed for each of the six focus groups, and a mixture of current students, staff and alumni were selected and trained to do the interviews. After the training a trial run was conducted. The designing of the questionnaires was difficult since we wanted to make sure that the questions would give us what we wanted to know without influencing the interviewees. We also wanted discussion through participatory action research. Clarity and objectivity were important criteria for us. The pilot project highlighted some weaknesses which we sought to correct with further training before the interviewers began the main field research.

Analysis

Having completed the main research, the next important step was to analyse and make sense of the raw data from the various constituencies. That was another stage where keeping our objectivity and vision before us was important. Unfortunately, not all the interview responses were recorded in the same way. Nevertheless, we recorded the findings in a draft research report, together with some preliminary ideas on the shape and content of the new curriculum. All this was shared with the faculty.

Results

From these discussions, a brand-new curriculum model, rooted contextually and relevant to the market – that is, the church – was designed and developed. The last step was to hold a two-and-a-half-day faculty workshop to work through the curriculum design process. Apart from dispensing with old courses and adding new ones, we also changed from a trimester to a semester approach. We have been surprised at how flexible the new framework is in that courses can be offered on a cyclical basis, such that students can join the college in any semester, and enjoy a range of elective courses. It has also been encouraging to realize that our home-grown curriculum model can be adapted to many other contexts outside Zimbabwe.

Conclusion

The scary thing is that we cannot blame the missionary now for any negative aspects of the curriculum, since we have developed it ourselves. Ownership brings with it responsibility. That is why we mentioned at the beginning that we are on top of the mountain, but scared. These are new waters for us as we learn about ongoing curriculum assessment.

We thank God for the opportunity to participate in this project, and we are grateful for the support rendered. Thank you, OCI and ICETE: you encouraged us to mature and be responsible for what we do and how we do it.

Stories of Our Journey
A Relevant Conversation

In February 2015, Dr Ray Motsi (TCZ President) presented a message at chapel showing how Paul's challenges in Galatians to rethink our worldview and to align it with Christ and Scripture (e.g. 3:1–4; 4:8–11) speak clearly to our Zimbabwean context. The African worldview and the Christian worldview are often at loggerheads. Syncretism is a major problem in the African church. This prompted us, as faculty, to draft a new curriculum model based on the transformation of worldviews (see appendix at end of chapter). From this, we developed a revised three-year BA Theology degree using worldview-based themes for each year. So all the courses in year 1 speak to the theme

"Approaching the Christian Worldview," with two underlying questions: *Where am I/are we coming from? Who am I/are we in Christ?*

The second year, with the theme "Advancing the Christian Worldview," explores this from a personal transformation, family and ministry point of view, looking at the implications for leadership and ministry. The third year, under the theme "Applying the Christian Worldview," explores the question *Where do we need to be?* through the twin lenses of church and society. These questions, to be addressed at personal, community and national levels, will be explored in each course offered in that year. By broaching the subject of addressing our African worldview, Dr Motsi unintentionally provided the idea for developing a key tool in the curriculum revision process.

How This Project Tied in with Other Things

About six months after we began the curriculum revision project in March 2014, TCZ made a decision to seek permission from the Government to charter as a private university because we felt recently required affiliation with another, local university would hamstring us in the long term. A sister school in Harare, the Harare Theological College (HTC), whose Board Chairman co-incidentally is a member of the TCZ Board of Trustees, expressed interest in joining with us in the university project. As discussions on that continued, their Principal and Academic Dean joined us in conversations on the revision exercise, and participated very meaningfully in the final workshop in April 2015 at which the curriculum framework was devised. The new BA program will thus be offered at both colleges, which will serve as the Harare and Bulawayo campuses of the Zimbabwe Evangelical Theological University (ZETU). At the same time, we also invited three other schools, Ekuphileni Bible Institute (EBI), Christian Open Bible School (COBS) and Rusitu Bible College (RBC), which are all offering the TCZ Advanced Diploma in Theology, to join us for the April workshop. This revision project was thus historical in that we are not aware of any other similar college in Zimbabwe having done something like this before; nor has it been done with five participating schools.

What the Research Revealed

To be honest, the research did not reveal any surprises. It merely formally confirmed what the faculty were already aware of. For instance, the call for other vocational training (e.g. electrics, building, carpentry) to provide income for pastors was not new. Though recognizing the rationale for this, the faculty felt such additional training would require extra staff and resources (equipment and material), as well as more time (at least a year) for the program. Furthermore, we felt it would duplicate efforts of institutions already offering such training more competently than we would be able to. Nor was the call for additional content in administration, leadership and counselling new either. These practical courses are presented at a basic level, but students and graduates often come to realize their value once the demands of ministry are experienced. Of course, more depth is always useful, and so an attempt has been made in the new curriculum to give more teaching hours to these three courses (at least ten extra hours for Counselling, and additional electives for Leadership and Administration can be added). Moreover, a new elective, Current Issues, intended as an interdisciplinary course addressing a range of ministry issues – both positive and negative – could also speak to related topics. More than the research itself, the informal interaction between the TCZ and HTC faculty provided scope for broader thinking and a honing of alternative ideas. The research prompted these conversations, and gave impetus to thinking "outside the box." Once a new curriculum model was devised – emphasizing the need to transition from the African worldview to the Christian worldview – the faculty began to realize the depth of change required. That realization, of course, is itself a journey for lecturers who now face the challenge of redesigning their courses to fit the new model rather than continuing with "business as usual." The revision, therefore, has resulted in a more contextually relevant BA program that, Lord willing, will begin to transform theological education in Zimbabwe. We hope to encourage other institutions to conduct their own research-driven revision projects in due course.

Discussion Questions

1. Two key elements of effective research-driven curricular change mentioned in the chapter are ownership and responsibility. For your own school, make a list of the different groups of people who need to have a sense of "ownership," and to what extent. And who are the key "responsible" people, and what are their different areas of responsibility?

2. TCZ encountered typical departmental "territorial battles." They overcame these through shared vision for the curriculum, as well as a level of compromise. To what extent do you anticipate comparable "territorial battles" if you were to implement curricular change at your school? Suggest some possible means by which these "battles" could be avoided or softened, so that change could be facilitated more smoothly.

3. The defining theme of the new TCZ is transforming its worldview, guiding the students on a three-stage journey of (1) approaching the Christian worldview, (2) advancing the Christian worldview and (3) applying the Christian worldview. Describe two or three ways in which you might apply elements of this strategic conceptualization in your own program(s) of study.

4. Due to capacity limitations TCZ was unable to respond to one of the key outcomes of the research: the call for other vocational training (e.g. electrics, building, carpentry) to provide income for pastors. This is a fairly widespread need in many parts of the world. Have you ever seen a program of theological study that was able successfully to integrate bi-vocational training? What were one or two of the key factors that enabled this program to work?

Appendix

Proposed Curriculum Model

Mission Statement: *To develop Christian leaders committed to effective leadership and ministry in both church and society.*

Underlying Philosophy

This model is predicated on a journey. It begins by exploring our human worldview and ends by setting goals to develop a Christian worldview. It begins in Year 1 by asking the broad questions: *Where am I coming from?* And *Who am I in Christ?* By "Approaching the Christian Worldview," human culture and worldviews are explored in contrast to being a new person in Christ. This is examined on three levels: Personally, Communally and Nationally.

As learners are introduced to college level study, courses would be presented through this dual lens, leading to self-awareness and exposure to what constitutes our current context. Hence, the emphasis in this year would be a seminar on the Zimbabwean situation, exploring the economic, social, political and spiritual state of the nation and the resultant ramifications for personal, communal and national spiritual and emotional well-being, and leadership and ministry. From this, together with a detailed exploration of the African worldview, as well as an introduction to the significance of a relationship with God, both of which will be referenced in all the courses, learners will be led through foundational subjects to prepare for their transformation during the rest of the journey.

In the second year, still on the journey and still considering worldview issues, the focus will be on "Advancing the Christian Worldview" through Personal Development (e.g. personal transformation, family and ministry issues). This emphasis will be presented through a "Positive Living" seminar in the first semester. The courses, again interconnected and/or integrated, will be presented with two aspects in mind: Implications for Leadership and Implications for Ministry. These will be considered from the twin views of Church (both "ordained" and "lay") and Society (marketplace ministry).

The third year, "Applying the Christian Worldview," will complete the journey by addressing the question: *Where do we need to be?* This will emphasize how a Christian worldview will apply on the three levels: Personally, Communally and Nationally, and from the twin perspectives of Church and Society. During the first semester, a seminar on financial literacy will equip students with skills in this area.

In line with the Bologna Process, the hidden curriculum elements of Chapel, Quiet Day, Discipleship and Mentoring Groups, Ministry, and Sports, together with other student activities, will be awarded credits. Learners will be asked to reflect on identified lessons related to and arising from these experiences.

Note:

- It may not be necessary to offer either extensive assignments or exams for every course; nor might every course take a full semester. This will reduce the workload for both students and lecturers.
- Courses may be offered as one-, two-, three- or four-hour or weekly modules, depending on the content and integration requirements.
- Since the courses will be presented through common lenses (worldviews, church, society, leadership and ministry, with the requisite annual questions), the material will be interconnected. Through each year, there will be major integrated research papers requiring learners to reflect on their discoveries. Learners will also be asked to develop Personal Learning Plans with their Advisors.
- The electives on offer in Year 3 are not yet finalized, and may in fact increase in number.
- A revised Ministry Practicum will be part of the second year.
- The third year will include a research thesis on a topic chosen by the student. This will build on the Methods of Research course and will require cross-disciplinary reflection.

- Four elective courses (two each semester over eight weeks) will be offered in a "track" system, allowing students to choose courses relevant to their intended area of ministry. There will be five tracks: Biblical Studies, Theology, Christian Education, Mission and Practical Theology.

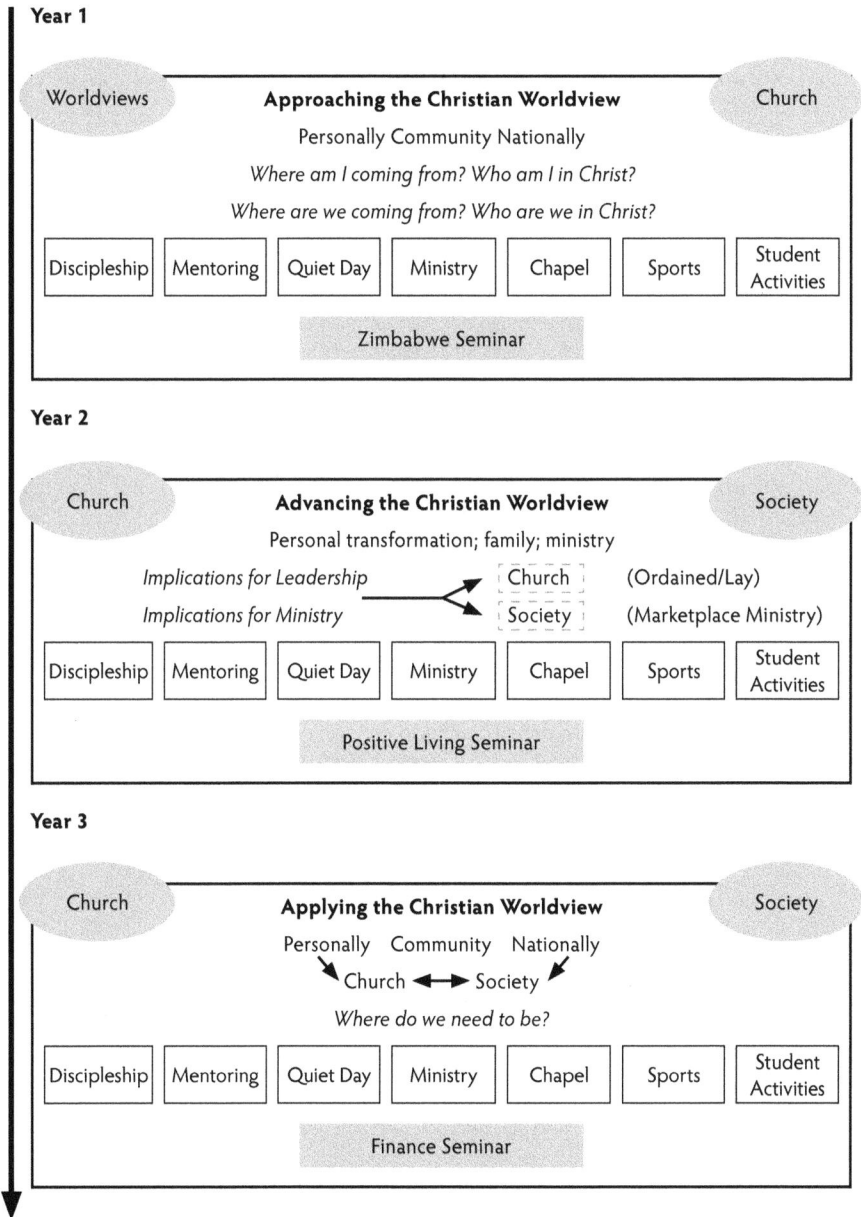

Year 1

Worldviews	**Approaching the Christian Worldview**	Church
	Personally Community Nationally	
	Where am I coming from? Who am I in Christ?	
	Where are we coming from? Who are we in Christ?	

| Discipleship | Mentoring | Quiet Day | Ministry | Chapel | Sports | Student Activities |

Zimbabwe Seminar

Year 2

Church	**Advancing the Christian Worldview**	Society
	Personal transformation; family; ministry	

Implications for Leadership → Church (Ordained/Lay)
Implications for Ministry → Society (Marketplace Ministry)

| Discipleship | Mentoring | Quiet Day | Ministry | Chapel | Sports | Student Activities |

Positive Living Seminar

Year 3

Church	**Applying the Christian Worldview**	Society
	Personally Community Nationally	
	Church ←→ Society	
	Where do we need to be?	

| Discipleship | Mentoring | Quiet Day | Ministry | Chapel | Sports | Student Activities |

Finance Seminar

8

A Sri Lankan Experience:
Some Surprising Outcomes

Lal Senanayake
Principal, Lanka Bible College and Seminary

Data gathering for the RDCR (Research-Driven Curriculum Revision) was a difficult experience, particularly in our "high context culture." In a high context culture the students will never say anything to offend the teachers even if they have something to share. They will not disagree with the teachers to their face. Since some of the senior faculty of LBCS conducted the interviews it was necessary for us to have a strategy to listen to the genuine emotions and experience of students.

Finding genuine data to learn the reality of the institute was important for its development. Therefore, we prepared our senior faculty for such a task. However, in this process we found that a collective response of the participants from each region would have brought better insights in a high context culture, because the group dimension helps in sharing thoughts and experiences boldly. In a group context, every individual in a high context culture feels emboldened to speak out. When we do our next research we will do it differently. After conducting one or two interviews we would revisit the interview questions. We would also revisit the interviewees for a second interview for clarification of areas which appeared to be ambiguous.

We are hoping that this RDCR experience is not the first and the last. LBCS has determined to continue to research and improve.

Surprising Outcomes

There were several surprising outcomes of the research. During the early stage, the team decided to involve independent interviewers for data gathering, because it was difficult for the faculty members to interview students in a high context culture and get genuine data. Since it was very costly to hire independent personnel, the faculty had to identify and find ways for how they should work on gathering data in a high context culture. This was a first-time experience for them, and it was encouraging to find that they did well.

The reason for success was that we had a series of meetings with faculty members to discuss who would work on interviews and data collection. I provided the background information regarding the cultural reality and the necessity for genuine data.

Another surprising outcome was that, as a result of the findings, the faculty and staff learned to look differently at the process of training at LBCS. It was an eye-opener for them to realize the impact of the implicit curriculum on the students.

It had been assumed that the overall performance of staff and faculty was up to standard until we listened to the experience of alumni of the institution. Most of the responses about the teaching at the faculty were positive. But the alumni (participants) said that they were not happy about certain conduct they observed. They said that what was taught in class must be seen in the real life outside the classroom. Most references were made towards particular attitudes of some staff members. The students had carefully observed the disparity between life and teaching. They made reference to a lack of love and concern from some staff members.

A further surprising outcome for most faculty and staff from the findings of the research data was that what we do in terms of training requires change and improvement. For example, faculty did not expect to hear about the necessity for broader integration – theory/practice, college/society and field ministry/ curriculum.

The Key to Success

The humility and commitment of the President, faculty and staff to learn from the alumni's learning experience at LBCS was the key to success. We were committed to finding real data, not the data that we would like to have heard. The qualitative research experience was fresh in my experience of learning at Trinity International University. I knew the power of qualitative research and therefore was determined to understand the real outcome of the research. The purpose was to develop the school for the glory of God and to see that LBCS training is making an impact on the church and society. Therefore, I motivated the research team to make sure that we found genuine data through the interviews.

What the Research Revealed for Our Seminary and Mission

- LBCS must be more intentional in broader integration, e.g. college/society, theory/practice, field ministry/curriculum. There is a realization that students are not able to make connections with society. The reason for this awareness is that LBCS conducted a series of seminars on the need for the integration of church and society. These seminars were held before the research process. The students realized the importance of this integration; hence, they shared that LBCS's training must be a model. For the previous ten years LBCS had stopped outreach missions with students due to heavy financial involvement. The students have realized the necessity for integration of mission and ministry, theory and practice into the curriculum.
- LBCS must be intentional about the integration of implicit and explicit curriculum. The interview participants felt that certain attitudes of staff did not match the explicit curriculum.
- LBCS must consider doing more of certain courses than is currently in the curriculum (more courses on management, leadership, counselling, sexuality and marriage, current social issues).
- There is a need for an ongoing education program for alumni. As a result of the findings, LBCS began to conduct seminars and workshops on certain selected topics, e.g. counselling, health care, mentoring, church leadership and financial management (financial stewardship).

- Library development is important. The library must be accessible from extension centres and ministry fields for alumni and extension students.
- It is important to listen to our stakeholders – customers.
- The review process must include staff, faculty and students as well as the leadership team of the institution.
- Precision is important in designing questions and tools for the research. For example:
    A. How did your *overall* learning experience at LBCS impact and shape your effectiveness in ministry?
    B. How did your time at LBCS help you (or not help you) to develop competence in ministry?
    C. How did your time at LBCS help you (or not help you) to develop your ability to foster strong, mutually beneficial interpersonal relationships?
    D. How did the modelling of the LBCS staff and faculty shape and influence your understanding of Christian leadership positively or negatively?
    E. How did your experience at LBCS affect the development of habits of discipline in your life?
    F. How did your experience at LBCS influence your interest in life-long learning in the area of theological and biblical studies, and in the development of effective personal Bible study habits?
- It is important to work together in designing tools for research.
- There is a need to meet more often as a team for consultation and discussion.
- It is important to meet participants in groups according to geographical location in order to get their collective response. This idea came up during the process of data analysis. The research team could only speculate what the outcome would have been had they planned for data collection in groups.
- The time limit for research was a challenge to faculty members with their other responsibilities. The research team was busy with the other activities of college, hence the process of evaluating data was slow. With other activities, it took nearly three months. It would

have been ideal to have at least six months for thorough processing and analysing.

- Having two interviewers was more effective than having only one.
- It is important to hold interviews in the students' own territory or geographical location rather than bringing them into the institution (high context culture).
- It is important to adapt to high context culture in the process.
- The interview process was too formal and appeared to be serious for the participants. To overcome this we had to keep the participants at ease by explaining the purpose of research development and improvement of LBCS's training program. Such clear orientation helped them to objectively evaluate their experience at LBCS. The other thing that could have been done was to employ a neutral party – non-LBCS person – to conduct interviews. Due to the limited budget LBCS could not do this. The context of the interviews was also important to set the participants at ease. The interviews were held in their own environment so that they felt free to express their experiences at LBCS during their time of study.
- The recording of interviews appeared threatening and was viewed with suspicion by the interviewees.
- The process of selecting participants ensured that both males and females were chosen.
- Participants should be intentionally chosen from different areas of the country.
- It was important to select those who could make honest contributions, who had the skill of analysing and evaluating their experience of learning at LBCS.
- There is a probability of being more successful if interview questions are revisited after one or two interviews.
- The selection of participants from different regions and ethnicities was helpful. The geographical and ethnic backgrounds of the participants were not taken into consideration during the process of analysis. The data revealed some unusual responses. For example, the church and the community had a better relationship with society in some geographical areas than they did in others. The ethnic

background also contributed to this. For example: in the regions where Tamils/Hindus were predominant, there appeared to be a better relationship between church and society. The communities where Sinhalese/Buddhists were predominant did not show a healthy relationship between church and society. This situation deserves extensive research, which may reveal reasons for it and suggest proposals for change of attitude.

- The process of research was complex, but was limited in terms of the deadline. These limitations caused difficulties for referring back to the participants for clarification on certain responses they had made. The data would have been richer if the interviewees had been revisited for clarification.

- For this reason, the factors of gender or geographical location were not taken into consideration in the research process. In the process of analysis, consideration of gender, ethnicity and geographical location may have brought more light into the findings.

Non-Faculty Staff Needed to Change

The Research-Driven Curriculum Revision (RDCR) program was conducted among students who had received training prior to the year 2010. According to the data received from interviews, the RDCR had direct ties to other things at Lanka Bible College and Seminary. Often the general assumption, at least in the Sri Lankan context, has been that only the faculty members of the institution provide the theological training to the trainees. It is assumed that the rest of the staff do not have any direct connection with or input into the program of theological training. The process and findings of RDCR revealed the importance of non-academic staff in the process of training.

The purpose of residential theological training is to provide a holistic training – mental, physical, spiritual, emotional and social development – for the students who join the institution. The college curricula have clearly defined course objectives in relation to development of human domains – cognitive, affective and behavioural (knowledge, attitude and skills). The purpose of learning a particular course must be to develop and bring about positive change and development in these three domains of the learner. The RDCR process revealed that such training must be a collective and collaborative effort by both academic and non-academic staff. The interview participants noticed an inconsistency between the teaching they received and how it is practised among the rest of the departments of the institution.

Students observed that certain "attitudes" of the non-academic staff were contrary to what they had learned in class. For example, the theory of leadership they learned in the classroom was contrary to some of the "leadership practices" they experienced within the institution. They observed "lack of collaboration" between departments. They also observed a kind of "impoliteness" from certain staff members towards the trainees. There were occasions when students experienced "lack of love and concern" in matters related to discipline. Students commented that some of the non-academic staff needed training in improving "attitudes, work ethics and social skills." Some students had been hurt by certain words the non-academic staff had used when working with them. Several incidents had shown the "disrespect" of one staff member towards another. This experience caused the students to question the gap between theory and practice.

Hence, the RDCR process helped the institution to reflect on some of these concerns outside the curriculum, and find ways of improving the attitudes and behaviour of the staff. These concerns have already been shared with the staff and faculty. Positive changes and development are clearly evident in these areas of concern.

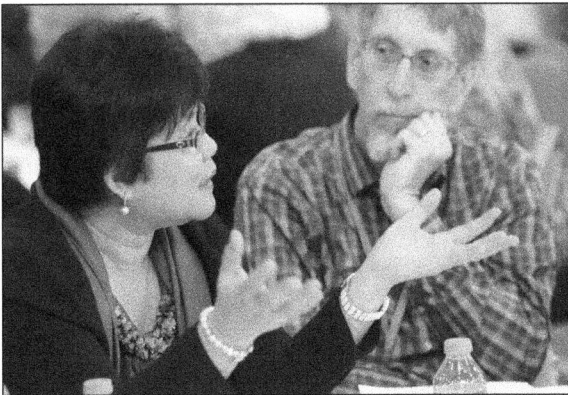

Discussion Questions

1. Lal's transparency in sharing the areas of change needed at LBCS has enabled meaningful growth in the quality of the school. Transparency and openness to criticism are always a challenge. Suggest one or two ways in which you might better promote transparency and openness to criticism at your school.

2. The greatest concern that arose from the LBCS research was a desire for better integration between college/society, theory/practice and field ministry/curriculum. To what extent do you believe that this sort of integration is a concern in your own programs? Describe some ways in which your school might better promote meaningful integration in one or more of the areas mentioned.

3. A second major issue was the disparity between life and teaching observed in some of the staff. As a result the LBCS needed to do intentional training of the staff in better reflecting the college's values. To what extent do your staff see themselves as "teachers" through their attitudes and actions? How might your school better promote a positive implicit curriculum through the way in which administration, staff, faculty and students relate to one another?

4. In retrospect LBCS found that their interview processes were too formal. To what extent do you think that this might be an issue in your own local context? What other cultural factors do you think might need to be taken into account to ensure quality data emerges from field research among alumni, churches and community leaders?

Section III

Issues in Change

If it was easy to change, we would just do it.

The ICETE 2015 Conference, and this book which comes from it, seeks to help seminaries to change. It is natural that there may be many objections and obstacles to embarking on this process. Indeed, some of the issues are raised in this very section.

The previous section gave accounts of how several seminaries have gone about researching their context and the outcome and impact of their graduates. In each case they had to overcome difficulties to do so. Some of the difficulties related to stakeholders, others to carrying out the research, others to conceptualizing a new curriculum, and others to implementing the changes that were driven by the research.

This section attempts to address some of the practicalities that seminary leaders will need to consider as they assess the readiness of their institutions to change, and as they go about doing research, and then reconceptualizing their curriculum and taking the bold step to change.

9

Leading for Change:
The View from the President's Office

Elie Haddad[1]
President, Arab Baptist Theological Seminary, Lebanon

The Arab Baptist Theological Seminary (ABTS) has become known as a place of innovation and a laboratory for experimenting with new ideas. Some of the major recent changes are a full curricular revision, and assessment for effectiveness. We are currently working on assessment for efficiency.

As we reflected on this period of major change, knowing that change is always difficult, it became obvious that the single most important factor that allowed change to happen at ABTS is a culture that has been nurtured over a number of years. Some think that for such innovation to take place the President needs to be the innovator. I believe that the main role of the President is to create and nurture an environment and a culture that encourage innovation.

In this short paper, I would like to highlight what are, in my opinion, the most important aspects of the ABTS culture that have made change possible, with the challenges that came with it.

Value-Driven Culture

One of the most important changes that took place at ABTS was consciously deciding to develop and nurture a value-driven culture: doing what we believe

---

1. Material first presented at OCI Institute, Amman, 12 March 2015.

is right rather than what has traditionally been done. Values started to shape our decisions, our decision-making processes, our structures and our relationships at an institutional level. This filtered down to the classroom and to all ABTS as a learning community.

We established overarching organization values, such as excellence, selfless dedication, integrity, respect, empowerment, interdependence, God-centredness and stewardship. These values govern our operation and our relationships. In addition, we established educational values that shape our curriculum, such as authentic worship, missional ministry, Christlike leadership, empowerment, reflective practice, community cohesion, and personal and spiritual development. These educational values became embedded in every class taught.

Challenges

This value-driven culture brought with it a set of challenges. It was most difficult at the outset. We started to make decisions based on values not knowing whether they would produce a better outcome. We had no precedent of looking at institutional life through that lens, and we could not find other models in our context to learn from. This was unproven ground. Obviously, people were sceptical, both internally and externally. It was not until this culture had the opportunity to prove itself that people came to believe in it, and ABTS became a model to follow in this.

Another challenge that this culture brought was that it proved to be costly. Integrity is costly in a place where things are normally done expediently while taking some moral shortcuts. But not just integrity. Our value system quickly moved us from a rigid system to a flexible system to meet the diverse needs of our community. Flexibility is costly as well.

Additionally, a value-driven community requires a minimum set of shared values among the community members. It becomes impossible to work with people within the community who do not share our core values. The shared values became our criteria for recruitment of staff, and for admission of students.

Members of the ABTS team: Elie Haddad, Rupen Das, Perry Shaw

Vision-Driven Culture

An important aspect of our ABTS culture is being vision-driven. Our vision always starts with what we, as a community, believe that God wants to do in our context. Our mission, thus, is what we believe God is calling us to do to accomplish that vision. God's mission for us, as we understand it, sets the criteria that we measure everything against. It is how we measure success and faithfulness. The vision and mission ethos permeate everything that we do at ABTS, from every staff member's job description to every course syllabus. This is an important lens through which we attract and retain people.

Challenges

As vision and mission are vital for ABTS, it becomes important to be able to discern God's vision and mission for us. Since discernment happens in community, the challenge is to be able to bring the right stakeholders into this collaborative process. The second challenge is to know how frequently this conversation should be revisited, given its complexity.

Being vision-driven and value-driven at the same time creates tension, a tension between having teleological and deontological perspectives. One is concerned with the ends and the other with the means. The challenge is to navigate institutional life while considering both perspectives, not as mutually exclusive but as equally important.

Culture of Empowerment

Empowerment is an important aspect of a culture in which innovation and creative change can take place. Empowerment means decentralized management and decision-making, the freedom to think creatively of options for improvement. A culture of empowerment attracts and retains leaders rather than followers, critical thinkers rather than conformists. It allows for every member of the institution to contribute to its mission. Everyone's voice is heard. Empowerment is accompanied by responsibility. Staff become accountable to strategic objectives rather than to specific tasks.

Challenges

When the growth in empowerment and distributed responsibilities is not matched by a solid accountability structure, that empowerment becomes a liability. This can quickly lead to misalignment. There has to be a clear system that ensures responsibility is matched with accountability, and that initiatives that emerge are aligned with the main institutional direction.

Another challenge inherent in this culture is the tendency to have power-plays within the institution. Power dynamics have to be managed carefully in this environment. In addition, there can be a sense of loss of control at the level of senior leadership. There will be decisions taken that senior leadership does not agree with. Trying to control all decisions will kill the spirit of initiative-taking. The challenge for senior management is to know how to navigate that.

Culture of Risk-Taking

No initiative can be taken without an element of risk. A culture of risk-taking encourages creativity and innovation. ABTS has become an experimentation laboratory for new ideas. We cannot be trailblazers and pioneers in new areas of education if we are not willing to take risks, knowing that many ideas will fail. A culture of risk-taking allows and supports new initiatives.

Challenges

Moving into uncharted territories has the inherent risk of failure. The challenge is to determine the level of risk that the institution is willing to take, knowing when to pull the plug on initiatives without discouraging initiative-taking.

Another challenge is the need to be able to navigate without a map, to press forward with a lot of uncertainty. This requires a high level of discernment to be able to make corrections swiftly.

Collaboration is also a challenge for institutions which are on the move. Collaboration is important among other small like-minded institutions. There is power in coming together and finding strategic synergies. However, for this to be manageable, collaboration needs to take place between existing traditional programs or systems. It becomes difficult to collaborate when one institution is moving in a new uncharted path.

Culture of Continuous Improvement

A culture of continuous improvement is crucial for change. Institutional maturity can come only through the desire to keep improving, doing things better, more effectively and efficiently, seeking excellence. If we want our institutions to remain relevant, we need to be responsive to our changing realities and changing context. We need to be responsive to regular feedback and evaluation. Change is costly. Continuous improvement is costly. However, the cost of not changing is much higher.

Challenges

This culture of continuous improvement brings with it many challenges. It can bring a sense of instability to the institution. Change is difficult. Continuous change is extremely difficult. Also, there is the possibility that change becomes a virtue in and of itself. The challenge then is that change may occur for the sake of change. There is the danger of revisiting the same issues over and over again.

With this culture comes also the challenge of assessment. If things are changing continuously and quickly, how do we know what we are assessing? It is difficult, for example, to assess the effectiveness of our curriculum if it keeps changing, if no two graduates have taken the same path.

Culture of Personal and Professional Development

A culture of personal and professional development requires the institution to be always on the lookout for new potential, to invest heavily in human resources and to develop leaders from within. Change can happen when we have our human resources prepared and equipped. This requires strategic thinking and succession planning.

Challenges

Developing people is costly, both in finances and in time. It requires a lot of patience to build capacity. The challenge is to balance between the immediate needs of the institution and the desired future needs.

Culture of Community

Change cannot be managed and led from behind closed doors. For the institution to remain effective and relevant, the whole community needs to be involved. A seminary does not exist in a vacuum. It exists to serve the church community. For change to go in that direction, the voice of the community needs to be heard. Change is a community journey, and can take place only through community ownership and support.

Challenges

To be able to include the community in all strategic discussions becomes costly and time-consuming. In addition, no one knows the potential and challenges of the institution as well as its staff and leaders. It takes specific skills to listen to the constituency and discern what is valuable feedback. The challenge is to build those skills and take the time to listen.

Discussion Questions

1. Elie Haddad sees the establishment of a value-driven culture as the starting point for building an innovative organization. What would you see as the key shared values in your organization? In what ways have these values been clearly articulated? How have you sought to encourage the community in sharing these values?

2. Describe one or two instances when decisions at your school were based primarily on financial expediency rather than on values. Given the limited financial resources of your school, how do you think these situations might have been managed differently?

3. Haddad sees the vision as being what we believe God wants to do in our context, and the mission being how we believe God is calling us to participate in the accomplishment of that vision. Take some time to reflect on the vision and mission statements of your organization. How might Haddad's understanding of vision and mission instruct your own understandings?

4. How do you seek to make the vision and mission statements of your organization more than mere "ink on paper"? How well are these statements

known by your administrators, staff, faculty and students? In what ways have you seen these statements function as lenses for decision-making?

5. What are some of the main factors that can make empowerment and risk-taking problematic in your organization? Describe one or two ways in which your organization promotes empowerment and risk-taking. How might these be strengthened?

6. Promoting continuous personal growth and organizational improvement is key to a healthy community. Describe some ways in which your organization facilitates personal growth and organizational improvement. Give at least one suggestion for how it might be done better.

10

What's It Worth?
Developing the Library

Melody Mazuk
International Consulting Librarian, USA

This might not be the title you expected for an introduction to thinking about principles and practices that will guide library development in the future. And yet it seems that this could be exactly the question we should be asking: What is it worth to have a library that will support the dreams and goals for theological education in our individual settings?

There are some principles that will help inform our thinking. Not surprisingly, the library development question cannot be looked at in isolation. Instead, it needs to be part of the larger conversation that also includes curriculum, faculty and location. The importance of clear, reliable and direct communication cannot be overstated.

Principle 1: It Is Impossible to Over-Communicate

One of the first practices that will enrich library development institutionally is to establish who has a seat at the table – that is, who are the individuals entrusted with decision-making capacity? Does the library have a strong advocate at the table? If there is no librarian within the institution, or the librarian is not at the table, does the library advocate have regular and reliable communication with the person who is responsible for day-to-day operations in the library?

Principle 2: The Library Serves to Support the Curriculum

The curriculum for present (and planned) degree programs is a key component to consider in library development. It is not only the content but also the delivery of the curriculum that needs to be taken into account. In order to develop regular, sustainable practices for excellent curricular support, the library needs to be made aware of decisions related to location, organization, delivery format. (See Principle 1.)

Principle 3: Context Is Everything; Or, It Really Is All about Location

Publishing has not kept pace with the change in the shift of population density in the Christian world, and libraries have not been able to keep pace with the rate of change in publishing.

Librarians, students and faculty want to be able to use materials that are contextually relevant to their specific situations, but the majority of published materials is still heavily Western. More often than not, the cost of printed books is prohibitive, and both the authors and the content of the books are reflective of their own contexts. It is not bad scholarship, but the question of relevancy cannot be ignored. A guiding practice in library collection development must include a focus on contextual relevancy.

The availability and accessibility of digital resources are topics driving library development conversations worldwide. There is no single correct or simple answer to the big question: Do we still need libraries? Instead, the question takes the form of a hydra: answering one question will often lead to at least two more, related questions. For example, should a library subscribe to an e-book lending plan or purchase individual e-titles? And if individual e-books are purchased, what platform is needed to read them? If a student has a computer but no Internet access, how will s/he be able to find, download and read e-books and journal articles? If a subscription to the print journal is cancelled in favour of accessing the journal through a database, what happens when the bill for the e-subscription cannot be paid? Is all back-issue access gone, or just current and future access? What happens when the lights go out (there is no electricity)? When an institution develops a policy about purchasing/lending/subscribing to e-resources, Principles 1 and 2 are invaluable. All constituent stakeholders need to be fairly represented.

Principle 4: Community Matters

Developing a library or a library collection is both a challenge and an opportunity. The opportunity to leverage resources through collaboration is at the heart of library work. As institutions worldwide look towards partnership agreements, one of the key questions should be whether the agreements extend to library usage. And when they do, who has oversight and responsibility for enacting the bilateral library usage agreements? If they don't, it would be wise to revisit the agreements (Principles 2 and 3).

Faculty: Are all individuals who teach courses on site? Or does the school also rely on visiting instructors? If visiting instructors are a regular part of course rotation, how is the need for materials to support their courses communicated to the library? And if the instructor is teaching remotely, what kind of library services are needed? (Principles 1, 2 and 3.)

Location: If a course or courses will be offered physically at more than one location, perhaps by more than one instructor, (policy) decisions need to be agreed upon about books or other materials that are made available to students on site. (Principles 1 and 2.)

Principle 5: Be Prepared to Ask for Help

There are people who embrace librarianship as a vocation and understand the work as their ministry. These people are often keen to serve as mentors and to work alongside or with individuals who have been appointed/assigned to work as librarians, both in a training and a mentoring capacity. They are often very fine dialogue partners in conversations about library staff training and stability, as well as the larger questions about library development.

Let's take a look at a few examples of some of these principles "in action."

Principle 1 often does not seem particularly helpful or necessary to those in charge of institutional planning and practice. In fact, it is likely the most ignored of these principles, when it could easily be the most rewarding. People are the very heart of an institution, and the more informed the constituency (students, staff and faculty), the more likely they are individually and collectively to be fully invested in the well-being of the institution and to be strong advocates and supporters. My oldest brother has a favourite saying that we family members have heard so many times over the years it has stuck in our minds: "I'd rather be looking at it than looking for it." Our dad was a plumber and my brother is an electrician. In both their jobs, being prepared for the unexpected often meant the difference between being able to finish a job and get running water restored for a family or heat and lights back on in the house, and having to leave a job unfinished and go back the next day, after "the part store opens," costing the unfortunate family even more money, not to mention inconvenience. How does this relate to Principle 1? you might be asking. A librarian is on the front line with students all the time, and to learn, for instance, from students that a course (or complete program) is being delivered online, rather than hearing that directly and well in advance from the Dean (this is a real-life example), is more than discouraging. The library staff is placed in the position of trying to find ways to make needed materials accessible to students and to do that without any additional funding or staffing support. Principles 1, 2 and 3 have just come together in this single example. "I'd rather be looking at it than looking for it" becomes a very real motto when printed or electronic materials needed for classes are not available in appropriate locations because the library staff had no idea the materials were going to be needed anywhere other than the home (main) campus. If the library had an advocate at the table, one who communicated clearly and regularly with the library staff, neither students nor faculty at extension sites would be disadvantaged by a lack of proper access. Lanka Bible College has been a participant in the Curriculum Revision Program and reported this as a part of their overall findings: Library must be accessible from extension centres and ministry fields.

"The library serves to support the curriculum" (Principle 2) is a blanket statement that also seems to be a statement of the obvious. It is so obvious, in fact, that the importance of the library gets overlooked in the academic planning stages. Many schools have an aspiration to expand their degree programs, and often the administration moves ahead with those plans without taking into consideration whether the library has adequate and sufficient resources to support the program. An interesting example of Principle 2 can be seen at

Nigerian Baptist Theological Seminary, which has a rather large enrolment in their current programs. According to their President, they do not have an adequate library collection at needed levels to support their existing programs. When asked what kind of library help they need, he had a list prepared:

- Five hundred new books to bring the library up to the needed level to support their *current* programs;
- Familiarity with Library of Congress Classification;
- Training in-house for library staff to learn to catalogue (classify) using Library of Congress;
- Assistance in integrating trained librarians who have no theological experience into the culture of a theological library.

In this example, both Principles 2 and 5 are well illustrated. A President who has both a strong commitment to and interest in the library and who recognizes the importance of the collection being able to support the curricular offerings is a wonderful advocate. A President who is proactive for the library and is not afraid to ask for outside assistance will be supportive of the library staff seeking assistance and asking questions (Principle 5).

Post-script: Community Matters – Or Location, Location, Location

This question of location has taken on heightened meaning in almost all conversations related to libraries, as the explosion of electronic resources has been almost overwhelming. It is not at all uncommon to hear something like this in institutional planning meetings, especially those related to budgets: "Why do we need a library any more, anyway? Everything is available online." Rarely are librarians invited into the conversation, and when they are, their voices are often not heard. Margot Lyon, of the American Theological Library Association, regularly reminds people, "Free doesn't mean without cost." It costs something to gain access to online materials, even if the only out-of-pocket costs are those related to actually getting online: a computer, a smartphone or a tablet, plus the (subscription) cost of being able to access the World Wide Web. Availability of access is growing more widespread each day, but it is by no means affordable or reliable in all parts of the world where theological education is being offered. Many theological materials that are "freely available" online are materials that are out of copyright, which generally means that the material is quite old and almost always written by Western authors, predominantly white and male. In other words, the materials may not be contextually relevant. And for those electronic resources that require a fee to access (ATLAS, for example), the cost of getting online and the speed with which something can be downloaded are also quite important considerations. Tyndale House's very innovative STEP (www.stepbible.org) is an online resource which makes serious Bible study software available free of charge. It can be downloaded either from the Internet (if a robust data connection is available) or from a flash drive, which Tyndale House provides free of charge.

As schools begin to explore the possibilities of adding extension centres or offering some or all of their programs online, these principles and questions about the library can enrich and expand the conversation.

Discussion Questions

Melody Mazuk proposes five key principles that inform the role of the library in theological education. Take some time to consider how each of these principles might impact your own school, giving one or two key responses to each of the questions raised:

1. "It is impossible to over-communicate." Who at your school is responsible for communicating the strategic value of the library and its needs? Describe one or two ways in which library communication might be strengthened.

2. "The library serves to support the curriculum." What proportion of the books in your library are directly related to the substance of your curriculum? How can you ensure continual monitoring of library usage?

3. "Context is everything." In what ways do you seek to make locally produced resources available to your students? To what extent might an e-library be appropriate for your school? How do you prioritize acquisitions and other library expenditure to maximize contextual relevance?

4. "Community matters." How are faculty brought into library decision-making? What relationships do you build with other local or regional libraries, perhaps including bilateral library usage agreements?

5. "Be prepared to ask for help." Who might be available locally or internationally to help your library staff develop their competencies?

Based on your responses to these questions, suggest two or three key actions that you believe your school should take in the next two to three months in order to strengthen your library in its service of your programs of study.

11

Practical Notes on Impact-Based Curriculum Development

Scott Cunningham
Interim President, Overseas Council USA

I n these notes, I'd like to outline a few topics regarding developing seminary based on an assessment of the ministry impact of the seminary's graduates.

1. There Are Different Ways Assessment of a Seminary (via Accreditation) Is Done

An article by Daniel Aleshire outlines different approaches to accreditation of seminaries which generally follow a chronological progression:[1]

a) Resource-based accreditation (1960s): Focused on assessing the resources of a seminary, that is, the input.

b) Mission-based accreditation (1980s): They are asked the question: Are the resources and the activities of the school sufficient to accomplish the mission of the school? Here the focus shifted from not only the resources but also the activities of the seminary.

---

1. Daniel O. Aleshire, "Fifty Years of Accrediting Theological Schools," *Theological Education* 49, no. 1 (2014).

c)   Evaluation-based accreditation (1990s): The seminary was asked to demonstrate how it was achieving its educational goals. Here the focus was on the output, particularly as seen in student learning.

The burden of this conference is that proper assessment of a seminary goes beyond evaluating the input (resources), activities and output of the seminary. We also need to assess the outcomes and impact of the seminary as seen in the graduates. This focus is consistent with what at least one ICETE agency has already stated in its standards. The Association of Christian Theological Education in Africa (ACTEA) standards state: "The institution should also develop procedures for measuring educational outcomes in terms of the actual achievements of its graduates, in order to obtain sound data against which to evaluate the appropriateness of its objectives and the effectiveness of its program."[2]

2. Why Aren't We Focusing on Outcomes and Impact in Accreditation and in the Assessment of Our Programs?

There are reasons why we generally have tended to focus on our resources and what we do in a seminary, rather than on the results of the seminary programs. While these reasons point to the challenges in assessing the results, they should not be considered obstacles which cannot be overcome.

a)   It is easier to count input and activities, as they are clear, defined, measurable. Results (outcomes and impact) are often less clear, less defined, less "countable." What exactly do you measure in a church that the seminary graduate now leads which would show the impact of the seminary's training on this graduate?

b)   Indicators for outcomes are not as clear. Do you count the number of people in a graduate's church?

c)   Sometimes it can take time for the results to emerge. It may take years for the graduates to begin to demonstrate all they have gained from the program, and even longer for the churches they are leading to show evidence of their ministry.

---

2. ACTEA, "Standards and Procedures for Accreditation at Post-Secondary Level" (1992).

d) It takes time and money to assess outcomes and impact.

e) Problem of control: we control what happens in the institution (input, activities, output), but we don't have any control over what happens after the graduate leaves the seminary. There are external factors which influence the outcomes besides the training which the graduate has received in the seminary. For example: the rural church where the graduate goes is being decimated by economic migration and is shrinking rapidly in numbers.

f) The problem of attribution: Can the success of this church under this graduate who is leading it be attributed to the training the seminary provided for this graduate? In almost all cases, seminary programs have only a partial influence over results as seen in the ministry of the graduate. External factors beyond the program's control influence the outcomes. This applies particularly to longer-term outcomes (remembering that it can take time for churches to change under a graduate's ministry). So there is the question of to what extent the results of the graduate's ministry can actually be properly attributed to the seminary's training or should be attributed to some other factors.

g) Seldom is there one cause for any particular outcome or result in the church or the community which the church impacts. There are more likely multiple cause–effect chains that influence and interact:

- This student might have done well in ministry no matter what training the seminary provided.

- What was the church like before this graduate came and what is it like now? Can the difference (either positive or negative) be attributed to the ministry of the graduate, or are there other factors?

- If the difference can be attributed to the graduate's ministry, what is it exactly about the graduate's ministry that has brought about this result? And how much of that can be attributed to the seminary's training? And what part of the training, specifically, has had influence (what courses, mentoring, etc.)?

3. A Focus on Results Is Not Only How We Should Assess Our Programs, It Is Also How We Develop Them

Programs of seminaries should be developed using the paradigm of "backwards design." That is, we begin with the end in mind. What is it that we want to accomplish? What are the results we want to see? From there, we ask questions about the best means (activities and then resources needed for those activities) to achieve those results.

a)   *Outcomes and Impact:* In designing our curriculum, we start with the outcomes we intend as a result of our program. We focus on the churches and Christian organizations which our graduates will lead and influence. What are the characteristics of a healthy church in our context?

b)   *Output:* Then we ask: What would the seminary graduate need to be, know and be able to do in order to facilitate the growth of churches with these characteristics?

c)   *Activities:* Then we ask: What kind of curriculum do we need to design that would likely form leaders with these characteristics? ("Curriculum" is broadly defined to include who is being trained, how and where they are being trained, who is training them, etc. It includes the explicit curriculum, extra-curriculum, implicit curriculum and null curriculum.)

d)   *Input:* What resources do we need in order to offer this curriculum? It is a mistake to start with "input," and yet that is typically how curriculum is designed. It is to our fault that we sometimes design curriculum starting with resources: What textbook do I have to teach this course?

4. Why Is the Focus on Assessment of Outcomes So Important?

Though it is challenging to do so, there are a number of reasons why assessment must shift from a focus on resources and activities to the results of our programs.

a)   *Because schools are no longer homogeneous.* They are more diverse in programs, in objectives, in mode of delivery. So different resources and activities are needed by different programs. It is not a one-size-fits-all standard.

b) *Because the things we often measure don't necessarily result in graduates who will make a positive difference in the church.* We all know of graduates who achieved straight As but make terrible pastors. We all know of schools which have wonderful facilities, libraries, funding and faculty with PhDs, but which are not making a positive change in our Christian communities (and not just because of their theology).

c) *Because we are accountable to stakeholders.* If you can demonstrate results, you can win support from your stakeholders. Donors are becoming more sophisticated – they want to know that their contribution is making a difference. Churches want to know that they can send their students with confidence that the seminary will provide the kind of training that will make a difference in the church and community. Potential students want to know that the time and money they are investing in their education will equip them to make a difference in their ministries. As seminaries we are stewards, entrusted with resources, students, and the mission of strengthening churches.

d) *Because assessment of results is the only foundation for improvement.*
   - If you don't assess results, you can't tell if you are achieving what you have set out to achieve. You can't tell success from failure.
   - If you can't see success, you can't reinforce it.
   - If you can't see success, you can't learn from it.
   - If you can't recognize failure, you can't correct it.

e) *Because it's the only way to know if we are fulfilling the mission of theological education and our seminaries.*

Consider the statements of two influential documents for evangelical theological education:

> 5. Continuous assessment: . . . Secondly, we must accept it as a duty, and not merely as beneficial, to discern and evaluate the results of our programmes, so that there may be a valid basis for judging the degree to which intentions are being achieved. This requires that we institute means for reviewing the actual performance of our graduates in relation to our stated objectives. (ICETE Manifesto on the Renewal of Evangelical Theological Education)[3]

---

3. ICETE, "ICETE Manifesto on the Renewal of Evangelical Theological Education," http://www.icete-edu.org/manifesto/.

Chris Wright's call for a "missional audit" of seminaries found its way into the Cape Town Commitment:

> We urge that institutions and programmes of theological education conduct a "missional audit" of their curricula, structures and ethos, to ensure that they truly serve the needs and opportunities facing the Church in their cultures.[4]

Discussion Questions

1. Under point 2 Scott lists a variety of possible reasons why we don't focus on outcomes and impact in accreditation and in assessment of our programs.

- Go through this list item by item and alongside each point rate whether for your school you believe the issue is (a) substantial; (b) evident but to a lesser degree; or (c) not an issue.
- Discuss your list with one or more other members of your school community. What issues stand out?
- Suggest at least one possible strategy for overcoming the barriers to a focus on outcomes and impact. How might your school take steps towards a healthier approach to assessment?

2. At point 3 Scott suggests that outcomes and impact should play a primary role in how we develop our programs. To what extent have your current programs been shaped by outcomes and impact, or are they more a product of traditional paradigms of theological education? Explain the bases for your evaluation.

3. In order for schools to move forward it is necessary first for there to be a shared vision for a focus on assessment based on outcomes. Find one or more other members of your school community. Now take the list that Scott gives at point 4 and use this list as a starting point for explaining to others in your community why assessment for impact is crucial to your school's faithfulness and fruitfulness.

---

4. Lausanne Movement, "The Cape Town Commitment" (2011), https://www.lausanne.org/content/ctc/ctcommitment.

12

A Critical Assessment of the Impact Agenda

Marvin Oxenham
Program Leader and Developer for Postgraduate Training
in Education, London School of Theology, UK

D istinguishing between different categories of impact is a good starting point for a critical assessment of the impact agenda of theological education. We have, on the one hand, *instrumental* impact, which can be subdivided in relation to (a) input and output, (b) impact on church and society and (c) impact related to competences, and, on the other, *intrinsic* impact. The ICETE C-15 Consultation engaged primarily with the first two subdivisions of instrumental impact, and we will here engage with the last two points, looking first at instrumental impact related to competences in the lives of graduates, and then at intrinsic impact that points us in a completely different direction and away from utilitarian ends, claiming that theological education is intrinsically valuable and should not be measured in terms of its missiological usefulness alone.

Impact Through Competences

A widespread trend in recent years has been to study competences to assess whether what is being developed by academics in schools matches up with what employers expect and with what graduates need in their prospective fields of occupation. Although there is a danger of competences driving out knowledge[1] and of a utilitarian view of education,[2] there is no denying that the complex realities that graduates face today demand not only complete knowledge but knowing competence. In the last decades, competences have become a key concept within the European Higher Education Area and are a central feature in the official documents of the Bologna Process.[3]

One very significant project that has been of direct inspiration to this research proposal is the 2000 Tuning Project, a Europe-wide consultation involving over 7,000 respondents, 101 universities and sixteen countries and including employers, graduates and academic staff/faculty in identifying the thirty most important competences that *all* degree programs in *all* subject areas of higher education should develop. A list of these competences can readily be found online,[4] and they include ability to work in a team, a spirit of enterprise, ability to identify and solve problems, basic computing ability and project management capacity, to mention just a few.

There are at least four advantages to assessing impact through competences. The first is that it represents an additional way of looking at output in the lives of students that goes beyond the knowledge and understanding that are typically caught on the radar screen of "grades," GPA, research output and transcripts. Second, it can enrich output evaluation and nuance it with dimensions of character education. This is because many competences are actually rooted in character traits and thus revive an ancient tradition of character education present since Paideia and largely lost through accreditation and academic captivity of theological education.

A third advantage of assessing impact through competences is that it reflects a commitment to listen deeply to the voice of society that we claim to serve. In assessing our impact, we must in fact ask whether society actually recognizes the impact we are trying to make or whether we are speaking

---

1. Mulder, Weigel, and Collins, "Concept of Competence," 67–88.

2. Teichler and Kehm, "Towards a New Understanding of the Relationships between Higher Education and Employment," *European Journal of Education* 30, no. 2 (1995): 115–132. JSTOR.

3. Mulder, Weigel, and Collins, "Concept of Competence"; Gonzales and Wagenaar, *Tuning Educational Structures in Europe – Final Report, Phase One*, 2003; Tuning Management Committee, *Tuning Educational Structures in Europe*, 2006.

4. Tuning Management Committee, *Educational Structures in Europe*, "Generic Competences," http://www.unideusto.org/tuningeu/competences/generic.html.

different languages and reflecting different values. Competence language gives theological educators a "fresh pair of eyes" that comes from engaging theologically with societal categories. If, for example, society is telling us that what is needed is individuals who are competent in decision-making, problem-solving and working in international contexts, we can demonstrate a recognizable impact in society by showing that *because* of our educational input our graduates are individuals who can make decisions, solve problems and work in international contexts.

Finally, competences represent a better measuring tool to assess impact in society. One of the major questions raised by the impact agenda is "How do we really know that theological education is impacting society?" Societal input is, in fact, problematic in proposed methodologies of measurement. Populations being surveyed about their impressions may be wrong or conditioned. Our data indicating whether "society is improving" as a result of theological education assumes an agreed definition of improvement, needs to deal with serious variables to know that it is actually theological education that has determined improvement and not other factors, and must include consideration of constraining factors and debilitating contexts.

In linking impact in church and society to the agency of theological education there may also a modernistic view based on a mechanistic ontology of reality operating in the background. This can lead to the (debatably wrong) assumption that if we get the curriculum right, we will always get certain results in society. But in a fallen world it may not be so simple. Assessing competences is a more realistic impact tool whereby we measure the impact of education on the individual and his or her relation to what is needed in society, rather than measuring the actual impact in society. So, for example, we realize that in a community that needs the capacity to generate new ideas and solve problems, we may not be able to establish whether that community has grown in this capacity and if theological education graduates have really made a difference, but what we can assess is the degree to which that capacity is important for the community and to what degree theological education is producing graduates with that capacity. Assessing competences thus proves to be a more modest approach as it does not tie itself into actually measuring change but is satisfied in producing curricula and graduates that are well matched in priority to the needed competences in current societies. If assessing only resources, input and output is too little, assessing impact in society may be too much. Assessing impact on competences sits in the middle.

There are many ways of measuring impact of competences in theological education and it is outside the scope of this chapter to list them, beyond an initial suggestion of three possible approaches. The first is to survey graduates at graduation and ask them to compare their competences on entry and exit which, when correlated, will allow an assessment of whether and where theological education has made a difference. A second possible approach is to survey graduates a few years after graduation and ask them about their competences on exiting theological education compared to those they have actually needed in life, society and work. This will diagnose whether theological education is making the right kind of impact. The third, and most complex, approach is to correlate surveys of graduates, academics and employers to gain a clear vision of overdeveloped and underdeveloped competences as well as the differences in perceptions and priorities of academics and employers.

Intrinsic, Non-Utilitarian Impact

In this second section I will argue that instrumental impact, however it is determined, is an insufficient metric for theological education and that intrinsic impact in which engagement with theology is seen as good in itself must be given a place. I will briefly mention a modern debate, then provide an ethical argument, an ancient primary source and a modern primary source, and finally conclude with a biblical narrative.

First the modern debate. There is currently a discussion raging in UK higher education as in 2014 the REF (Research Excellence Framework) responsible for funding research in HE included "impact" as a significant element in the framework criteria. In brief, the kind of research that is most likely to get funded and classified as "excellent" is research that brings about positive impact on society and economy. Debates have included issues around measuring the sheer complexity of how research actually makes impact, the discrimination among disciplines, the downplaying of work that is exploratory and theoretical and the spectre of prioritizing lower- over higher-quality work. This is all to say that the utilitarian assessment of education is framed within a broader contentious debate.

My ethical argument looks to ethical theories to find answers to the question: what makes theological education "good" and of value? Two main theories will assist us: the first is utilitarianism and the second deontology. A utilitarian, instrumental judgment of theological education will claim that theological education (as any other object of action) has value if it is useful. Theological education therefore is good if it leads to a better society and to making the world a better place, and if it serves the purposes of welfare, utility and fitness for purpose. Typical utilitarians would include personal happiness, pleasure and well-being as measures of good, but as evangelicals we tend to shy away and prefer missiological measures. But here looms the question: do our missiological commitments restrict our vision of theological education to a strictly utilitarian set of judgments? If we look at the mission statements of our colleges they are about transforming church and society, about moving God's kingdom forward, about service and training leaders. But what are we really saying? Are we saying that what is worthwhile is what serves others and the world, and that even areas like spiritual formation that may benefit our students during their studies are really instrumental to the outward benefit of the church and world? If this is so, then it appears as if theological education is elegantly commodified to the market of Christian service where the missiological GDP of the kingdom is the main assessment parameter.

But there is something missing in this picture, as becomes apparent when we take a deontological view that links good to duty (the root "deon," meaning "one must"). This view suggests that educating theologically is a duty because it is right and therefore that it is good regardless of whether it leads to a better society, to making the world a better place or to any instrumental purpose. Theological education is simply the fitting thing to do in this world, rooted in ontology and the dutiful relationship between human beings with a rational mind and receptive spirit and a revealing God who wishes to be known. As Kelsey reminds us, theological education is basically about theology – the understanding of God. Of the different assumptions of what it is to understand God listed by Kelsey, perhaps the way of contemplation, in which fulfilment of human life is disengaged from any sort of political life and contemplation of "real reality," is one that most of us would endorse in our theological schools.[5] Contemplation and knowing God thus appear divested of any instrumental use and loom large as basic creature duties.

Intrinsic impact, contemplation and knowing God as a basic duty call into question hierarchies between *theoria* and practical and productive understanding, and here we turn to an ancient source and in particular to Aristotle. Not enough can be said in fact of the impact of Aristotle on the shape of education in Europe as his *Lyceum* was destined to become the main model for both Greek and Roman education and then later for medieval European universities that in turn have served as templates for much theological education. The curriculum in the *Lyceum* featured a rigid disciplinary hierarchy, for Aristotle ranked knowledge in terms of three sciences: *theoretical, practical* and *poietical*.[6] Of these the *theoretical* sciences ranked highest as they had to do with the pure contemplation of truth, which included metaphysics, physics and mathematics (it is important to note that physics and mathematics were studied without any practical relations to life but as pure facts of harmonious reality to be contemplated). The *practical* sciences, namely ethics and politics, ranked second as knowledge that could guide human action, and the *poietical* sciences ranked last, because they were the knowledge of doing, representing the disciplines that were farthest from contemplation and closest to the concrete preoccupations of life. This hierarchy rests on the basic question of human identity,[7] concerning which Aristotle claimed that the most distinguishing feature of human beings is their rational soul. It follows that, if rationality is what makes human beings different from animals, the love of knowledge and the search for truth are the highest functions of human life. This basic syllogism explains why theoretical knowledge is uppermost in Aristotle's curriculum and why the primary concern of education was rational contemplation and not the acquisition of scientific knowledge.[8] Learning for Aristotle was therefore not an

---

5. David H. Kelsey, *To Understand God Truly: What's Theological about a Theological School* (Louisville, KY: Westminster/John Knox, 1992), 35.

6. Trombino, *La Filosofia Greca Arcaica e Classica* (Bologna: Poseidonia, 1997), 336.

7. In the *Protrepticus* the young Aristotle lays out an anthropological stance that would deeply influence Cicero, Augustine and many modern thinkers.

8. Plato similarly prioritized philosophy (dialectic) as the supreme study, followed by the study of the sciences that would provoke reflection and lead to the ideal world, and then, lastly, by the training of the body. The chronological order was important for Plato, beginning with bodily training of children, training in the sciences for youth and, finally, dialectic. Progression from one

instrumental means but an activity of intrinsic value that led to *eudeaimonia* – human happiness. According to Aristotle, the more we abstract in metaphysical theory, the more we are human. To seek truth for itself, with no further/exterior motives, is the final end, "that which is always desirable in itself and never for the sake of something else."[9] Theoretical education, according to Aristotle, will lead to happiness because it is desirable in itself and can be seen as that which is "final without qualification." Applying this to theological education, one would conclude that to *see* God ranks higher than to *serve* God.

We turn finally and briefly to a contemporary source featuring taxonomy of existing educational goals: *Educating for Shalom* by Nicholas Wolterstorff.[10] Although it is not related specifically to theological education, one can easily make the connection and see that, of his six goals, three could be classified as instrumental and three as intrinsic. Among the instrumental goals we find the *Christian service model*, in which we train students to enter Christian service; the *socialization model*, in which we equip students (especially the poor) to contribute to utility and to the welfare of nations and communities; and Wolterstorff's *Shalom model*, in which we challenge, nourish and equip students to address the wounds of humanity in a prophetic vision of shalom. The three broadly intrinsic goals instead include the *Christian humanist model*, in which we initiate students into the cultural heritage of humanity to make them flourish; the *maturation model*, in which we create free spaces where students can discover and become un-indoctrinated individuals; and the *academic discipline model*, in which we introduce students to objective theoretical knowledge of the workings of the world and thus fulfil a cultural mandate. There is no space here to engage with each of these models or to apply them to theological education in particular, but the taxonomy in itself makes a point, namely that the assessment horizon is broader than single models of instrumental measurement.

So what should we conclude? Should we try to assess which of Wolterstorff's models is the right one? Need we engage with Aristotle to determine whether

---

level to the next was subject to distinction in character and mind and fitness for higher studies.
9. Aristotle, *Nicomachean Ethics*, in B. Jowett, *The Works of Plato & Aristotle – 35 Works* (C&C Web Press, 2009), Book I, 7. Ebook.
10. N. Wolterstorff, *Educating for Shalom: Essays on Christian Higher Education* (Cambridge: Eerdmans, 2004). Kindle.

theory is truly higher than practice and societal impact? Should we privilege deontology and duty to know God over utilitarian service to our neighbour? Should we skew any instrumental impact agenda in favour of intrinsic values at the risk of becoming self-referential and irrelevant in our world? The well-known biblical narrative of Martha and Mary with Jesus found in Luke 10 provides a framework for these questions. We have here two women, one active and one contemplative; one perhaps looking for instrumental impact, and the other, for intrinsic impact. Which of these two women is "right"? The answer is that both were right, for both women were loving Jesus. Although, to be fair, the weight of the narrative actually has Mary winning the day, we should be cautious in transforming this narrative into a normative, for Jesus is responding to Martha's complaint based on her wrong hierarchy, and so paradoxically reverts Martha's hierarchy to enhance the value of Mary's approach. We would, however, be hard pressed to argue that Scripture normatively has this kind of hierarchy (or any hierarchy, indeed). We simply have both. As the ICETE C-15 Consultation on the Impact of Theological Education has been largely a "Martha conference" focusing on instrumental impact, this is a "Mary paper" that reminds us of the depth and breadth of our horizons.

Discussion Questions

Marvin's article focuses on two areas that have not played a central focus elsewhere in the Assessment for Impact Project: instrumental competences and intrinsic value. Both of these are significant considerations.

1. How might the "instrumental" and "intrinsic" aspects of education be seen as mutually complementary in theological education?

2. Make a list of competences that you believe are appropriate for your own particular program(s) of study. Share your list with those of other members of your school community.

3. Consider the suggested means for assessing competences that are given in the final paragraph of the first section. Which of these approaches do you believe your school does well? Suggest at least one possible way in which the competences of your program(s) might be assessed more effectively.

4. In what ways and to what extent do you believe that "intrinsic" aspects are evident in the approach taken to theological education at your school? How is *shalom* nurtured in and through your students?

13

Culture, Communication, and Research on Impact

Perry Shaw
Professor of Education, Arab Baptist Theological Seminary, Lebanon

One of the most innovative features of the recent Overseas Council Assessment Project has been the diversity of cultural contexts in which the work has been completed. Because the research was completed at a local level by local leaders, a wide range of approaches was taken. In a unique way, each approach was able to solicit meaningful information that could help shape curricular review. This diversity emphasizes a key principle: meaningful research on impact is profoundly coloured by culture.

The unspoken and often unconscious assumption that the West is best and normative is seen in the emphasis of many Western-based international organizations on metrics and quantitative research – in some cases linked to funding. Frequently these organizations offer their services by bringing a Western research group into a non-Western context. The very extensive data and numeric results that are generated can be quite impressive in appearance but in point of fact are often largely meaningless, because cultural factors have rendered them meaningless. When a theological institution conducts its own research on impact it should choose the methods that best yield the most meaningful results for the context.

High Context and Low Context Communication

The key to understanding the relationship between culture and research methodology is the foundational difference between the ways in which people communicate. While multiple factors shape communication patterns, one helpful lens is the distinction between what is known as high context communication (HCC) and low context communication (LCC).

The terms "high context" and "low context" communication refer to the extent to which meaning is embedded in the context itself, and not merely in the words. In HCC societies the context is all-important. Words are not seen as the primary vehicle of communication. Rather it is the context within which words are spoken – and most particularly the non-verbal components – that delivers the message. In LCC societies the context carries far less value. The meaning is carried primarily in the actual words. You say what you mean, and clarity of speech is seen as a great virtue.

The following slightly adapted true story illustrates the difference between high context (indirect) communication (HCC) and low context (direct) communication (LCC) cultures.

> In a Bible college in the West students came from all over the world. One particular year two young women – one from China (Chen Su) and one from the Netherlands (Cornelia) – were asked to share a room. Within a week both students came to the school's Dean of Women asking to be placed elsewhere. "Chen Su is a habitual liar," said Cornelia. "She never answers my questions, and always smiles and says that everything is all right when I know that there are things I do which irritate her. I tell her openly when things she does irritate me – but she refuses to do the same. Why can't she just come out in the open and tell me?" Chen Su, on the other hand, told the Dean of Women, "Cornelia hates me. It seems that everything I do is wrong, and she is so blunt. I listen and try – but it is not good enough. And when I say that it might be difficult to do something, she doesn't realize that it is my way of saying 'no': I can't tell her straight out – this would be so aggressive and offensive."

As is common, this story illustrates how people from HCC societies can often view LCC communicators as aggressive, insensitive and impolite. People from LCC societies may view HCC communicators as deceitful and incomprehensible.

Some of the key differences between HCC and LCC are shown in the table.[1]

	High Context Communication	Low Context Communication
Information location	Most of the information is either in the physical context or internalized in the person	Most of the information is vested in the explicit code of the actual words spoken
Quantity in communication	Speakers prefer to provide the least amount of information, and listeners are expected to be able to infer meaning and intent	Speakers aim not to give more *or* less information than is necessary
Obscurity and ambiguity	Speakers tend to use ambiguity as a means of communication	Speakers endeavour to avoid obscure expressions, ambiguity, excessive verbosity and disorganization
Precision in communication	Tends to be imprecise	Tends to be precise
Type of word use	Use of qualifier words such as "maybe," "perhaps" and "probably"	Use of categorical words such as "certainly," "absolutely" and "positively"
Relationship between communication and feelings	Speakers are expected to communicate in ways which maintain harmony in their in-groups, perhaps transmitting messages that are inconsistent with their true feelings	Speakers are expected to communicate in ways which are consistent with their feelings
Silence	Silence is a communicative act rather than a mere void in communication	Silence is space to be filled
Dealing with conflict	More likely to assume a non-confrontational, indirect attitude towards conflict	More likely to assume a confrontational, direct attitude towards conflict

1. Adapted from W. B. Gudykunst, "Individualistic and Collectivistic Perspectives on Communication," *International Journal of Intercultural Relations* 22, no. 2 (1998): 107–134.

There are two types of HCC: elaborate and succinct. In elaborate HCC societies (such as the Middle East) there is a high quantity of talk, most of which is designed to affirm the other and build relationship. For example, in a situation of conflict between two Arabs over the cost of painting an apartment, the first forty-five minutes were spent with the landlord telling the tenant all the reasons why his family were the best tenants that had ever occupied the apartment, and the tenant saying that the landlord was the best his family had ever had. Then came about three minutes in which the landlord said, "We love you so much that there is no need to pay anything, for what is $600 between friends?," and the tenant thanking the landlord for his generosity. The two parties then spent another fifteen minutes drinking coffee and affirming each other, both knowing that the settled price was $600. Much talk – with only a couple of sentences in which the substance of the meeting was communicated. More important than the management of business was the communication of relationship.

East Asians, on the other hand, have succinct HCC: it is in the form and timing of silence that much communication takes place. Very often the most powerful person in decision-making is the one who speaks least, and the essence of the communication may come in a slight nod from the major power-broker. In all forms of HCC cultures territory is all-important: the person in whose home the communication takes place carries the greater power.

Monocultural people from each of HCC and LCC cultures can easily misinterpret the intent and nature of the other. Consequently I have more than once heard a Westerner describe all Arabs as "liars" because they say one thing when they mean something else. I have likewise heard Arabs describe Westerners as rude, arrogant and offensive because they don't show appropriate honour and respect to other people, and their forthright speech breaks relationships. In each case the perception is one rooted in measuring another's communication style based on one's own.

In that the Scriptures were written in the HCC environment of the Middle East, it is not surprising that there is a predominance of HCC styles evident in the Bible. But it is striking that there is also a call to greater clarity in speech than is the norm in HCC situations: "Let your yes be yes . . ." That said, neither LCC nor HCC can be said to be more "biblical" than the other. Each has its strengths and weaknesses, reflective of both God's character and the fall.

Context, Communication, and the Use of Qualitative and Quantitative Research

With the contrast between LCC and HCC as a framework it becomes evident why in HCC situations metrics and quantitative research have limited meaning and value, and the preferred means to assess impact is qualitative.

If a Westerner were to come into an Eastern context, the Easterner will do all in his or her power to please the Westerner. Consequently, and particularly in the case of surveys, numerics will almost inevitably provide a glowing portrayal of the program being assessed, irrespective of what the participants actually think. More than once I have seen Western ministry programs come into the East, concluding with an evaluation survey, the results of which the Western leaders take at face value, missing the key hints and overtones that actually pointed to a very negative evaluation.

In general, qualitative research through face-to-face interviews is far more effective in HCC situations. Because of the unique communication styles found in each cultural context, meaningful data can emerge only if the style of the research and the processes by which the data is analysed are done by locals.

In the Overseas Council Assessment Project the local nature of quality research was repeatedly seen. Perhaps the starkest contrast in the Project was between the work done in Argentina and that done in Sri Lanka. In the relatively LCC situation of Argentina, the predominant use of quantitative surveys was extremely appropriate, generating statistical data that was able to shape meaningful and relevant actions. In contrast, the cultural setting of Sri Lanka is HCC, particularly in the rural and largely oral communities served by most of the graduates of Lanka Bible College and Seminary. In such a context quantitative surveys would have been meaningless – even if obtaining survey responses was possible. Wisely, LBCS chose a qualitative approach, and trained interviewers to go out into the territory of the interviewees to conduct the survey in the form of relaxed open conversations. The results generated were equally profound and valuable as those gained in Argentina, precisely because the methodology, implementation and analysis were all undertaken by local experts who understood both the nature of quality research and the contextual realities.

It was also noteworthy in the Project that participating African schools often employed a methodology of gathering *groups* of people together to talk around open-ended questions – a form of group-generated qualitative research that was appropriate and significant for an environment that is both HCC and highly communal. Again, the results of the final analysis were insightful and invaluable.

Towards Understanding

How, then, should funding agencies (predominantly located in the LCC cultures of the West) develop appropriate accountability and quality assessment to guide them in relating to schools in HCC cultures? I believe the key is to find cultural interpreters – people who understand both LCC and HCC cultures and can be a bridge to bring meaning between people from these two cultures.

Some time ago I was talking with another Australian who has served in the Middle East for over thirty years, and we were bemoaning the failure of so many intercultural teams, despite the growing desire for such teams in global missions. As we talked we discovered that virtually every successful intercultural team had a leader who had lived in each of two or more culturally distinct contexts for at least ten years. It is only with time that a person is able to recognize both the strengths and the weaknesses of his or her culture of origin and of another culture.

I would suggest that quality intercultural interpreters likewise need longevity in both LCC and HCC cultures in order to help people from each of these cultures to understand the other. Such bi-cultural people are a rich resource for helping both funding agencies and financial recipients to find means of developing research and information that is culturally sensitive to people from both HCC and LCC cultures.

Conclusion

There is no question that a culture of assessment is increasingly being embraced in theological education around the globe. As this desire for allowing assessment of impact to shape curriculum grows, it is imperative that Western agencies not present Western methodologies as normative, with other methods as somehow substandard.

The best method is not the Western method. The best method is the one that takes seriously local patterns of communication and shapes the research accordingly. Consequently, meaningful assessment practices need to be developed locally, implemented locally and analysed locally, so as to ensure that the results generated are valuable for what God is doing locally.

Discussion Questions

1. To what extent do you see high context and/or low context communication worked out in the cultural setting of your own program? Please give one or two specific examples to explain and justify your perspective.

2. Give one or two specific ways in which different understandings of high or low context communication might shape the way that impact assessment should take place in your program's cultural setting.

14

What Difference Do We Make?

Impact-Based Assessment

Elizabeth Sendek
Rectora, Fundación Universitaria Seminario Bíblico de Colombia

Historically the mission of institutions of higher education (post-high school) was the acquisition, preservation and dissemination of knowledge. The generation of knowledge, understood as scientific research, was added in the nineteenth century. In the twentieth century, the mission of universities was further expanded to be not only centres of education and discovery, but also "engines of economic growth, beacons of social justice and laboratories for new modes of learning."[1] Through these functions, schools related to diverse social groups.

In many countries colleges and universities are expected to justify the extent of their relevance and effectiveness in terms of the contribution of their graduates to the economic development of the nation. Thus the analysis of the relations between higher education and the marketplace has become prominent in the agenda of these institutions. Efforts to understand this relationship have led educational institutions to adopt mechanisms through which the quality of educational programs is verified through the performance of its graduates.

---

1. "Higher Education: The University Experiment," *Nature: International Weekly Journal of Science* 514 (15 October 2014): 287, accessed 10 November 2015, http://www.nature.com/news/higher-education-the-university-experiment-1.16133.

Follow-up or tracer studies have become fundamental to this end. Most of them are influenced by the human capital approach that sees education (formal and non-formal) as part of the marketable skills in which workers make an investment for the purpose of being productive in the marketplace.[2]

An example of this is the recent Indicators Model to Evaluate the Quality of Education (MIDE) designed by the Colombian education authorities to rank institutions, colleges and universities, introduced in 2015. It follows the pattern of the Academic Ranking of World Universities, known as the Shanghai Ranking. Six dimensions of life in a school are assessed: students, graduates, faculty, research, retention and outside financing, and internationalization. For each dimension several variables are taken into consideration, so the complete evaluation includes eighteen factors. When assessing the impact of graduates, the factors considered are occupation index, entrance salary, advanced degrees, innovation (patents registered under their name, artistic production), membership of scientific associations, scientific or professional awards, and positions held in national or international organizations.

As one examines all eighteen factors, it becomes clear that not one addresses the notion of ethics in a country where most sectors recognize that a key detrimental factor in the economic and social development of the nation is corruption. This is deeply disconcerting because this model was developed for a nation where more than ten anti-corruption agreements have been signed in the public and private sectors during the past five years, where 94 percent of businesses state that bribes are usual, 24 percent admit to having bribed a government official and 87 percent of the population thinks that public officials are corrupt,[3] and where CEOs of the largest private employers of university graduates have stated that the number one characteristic they seek in new employees is an ethical posture. This points to the missing connection between an assessment model of higher education and the realities and needs of the context in which that education takes place.

---

2. Daron Acemoglu, *Lectures in Labor Economics*, ch. 1, "The Basic Theory of Human Capital," accessed 30 October 2015, http://econ.lse.ac.uk/staff/spischke/ec533/Acemoglu%20Autor%20chapter%201.pdf, 3.

3. *Pacto por la transparencia en el Día Nacional contra la Corrupción*, El Espectador, August 17, 2017, https://www.elespectador.com/noticias/bogota/pacto-transparencia-el-dia-nacional-contra-corrupcion-articulo-579808. Accessed 30 Sep 2015. Translation mine.

This raises the question of what should be different when assessing the engagement and effectiveness of formal theological education. Of course we need to speak the language of formal education, but we also need to speak the language of theology. This is not so we can have two different discourses to please two different audiences, but in order to articulate one discourse, true to the dual nature of our particular calling. We need not only to learn the language of impact assessment as it relates to education, with its focus on the ministerial career and fruit of our graduates, but also to speak that language with a strong theological accent.

During the conference convened in Antalya we were exposed to the rationale for impact assessment in theological education, to methodological approaches for the process and to case studies. Yet the language of impact-based assessment of our formal programs begs for a revision of accreditation standards when it comes to alumni follow-up. The accreditation manuals of most ICETE affiliates refer to the relationship between schools and their graduates mostly in terms of continued contact, placement, support for the school and ongoing support for their ministry. If, after this conference, we are convinced of the importance of identifying impact for assessment purposes, criteria that invite taking outcomes into consideration should be formulated and included in the accreditation processes.

For those of us who depend on government accreditation of our programs and institutions, it should mean learning to express the relevancy of our existence in terms that show how our output connects with the needs of society and the difference that makes. When submitting one of our theology programs for accreditation by the Colombian authorities, this is how we, at the Biblical Seminary of Colombia, argue our case:

> We recognize that this is not a professional field that responds [directly] to a particular need for the economic development of the country. Our mission is to contribute to the development of the social fabric of society. Our profession of the Christian faith acknowledges the church as an important agent of society, an agent that constantly enriches the fabric of society.
>
> The ethical behaviour of our graduates nurtured by their faith commitment, and of those they influence through their

professional service, should contribute to one of the goals proposed by the national and local governments: the reduction of corruption. This reduction will have a direct impact not only on the economic reality of the country, but on all dimensions of society.

The theological accent should be clearly audible as a clear sign of our identity. In our bilingualism, the absolutist demands of the academic and educational discourse should be superseded by the truly absolute demands of faith.

The Antalya conference reminded us, evangelical theological educators from around the world, that the impact in terms of God's Project (the macro-curricular framework of our educational activity) rests on faithfulness to his everlasting revelation (the central content of our teaching) and on incompetence that leads to humility and dependence upon the Almighty, whom we serve and in whose name we teach others.

I would like to propose that in determining the effectiveness of our programs, the opinions of our own graduates and the expectations of their employers, their congregations and their neighbours, should have less weight than the following three questions, based on the charge made by God against the professionals of religion in Israel in the days of the prophet Hosea, when they had become corrupt by devoting themselves to something radically different from the essence of ministry:

1. *What do they proclaim?* Do they proclaim God's Word and not what people want to hear (Hos 4:1–4)? We can educate church bureaucrats, skilful in the use of religious discourse, which may even disguise idolatry, but lacking in the knowledge of God.

2. *What do they seek?* Are their ambitions fame, power, riches – or God's glory? We have an endless capacity to seek recognition in and of what we do instead of celebrating powerlessness (4:7).

3. *How do they live?* Do they exhibit corruption, abuse of others and immorality – or passionate love for others (6:9)?

The technical processes and tools that were shared in the conference are helpful. Yet the impact of the sacred requires that we stubbornly preserve the prophetic role of theological education (formal and non-formal), refusing to shape our programs to produce church bureaucrats with marketable skill:

accomplished in the formulation of religious discourse (that disguises idolatry and heresy), and innovative and effective in the use of religious techniques (while lacking in the knowledge of God and the ethical behaviour that reflects his character and love). Our engagement and impact should be assessed by how the life and the fruit of our schools reflect faithfulness, love and acknowledgment of God (Hos 4:1).

Discussion Questions

1. Elizabeth Sendek points out that the assessment process necessitates an associate advocacy for changes in the understanding of accreditation. This is particularly challenging when engaging with secular government accreditation. She cites an example whereby the Biblical Seminary of Colombia appealed to its role of building the "social fabric" and the "reduction of corruption." Using Sendek's sample as a model, write a short piece as though to the Ministry of Higher Education in your country, in which you justify one or more of your own programs as significant for service to the community.

2. Sendek urges three essential questions that need to be brought to bear on a college's alumni when assessing theological education: (a) What do they proclaim? (b) What do they seek? (c) How do they live? For each of these essential questions, briefly explain some processes whereby you might:

- assess the extent to which your graduates are responding to these questions in an appropriate and healthy way;
- ensure that these questions are shaping the ethos of your school and the structure of your curricula.

Postscript

The hegemony of the Western theological tradition in the Majority World is being challenged in many ways. This is true of both content and method. One could argue that it has not only limited the Majority World from addressing its own multiple questions in its own multiple ways, but it has also ceased to serve the Western world. As the West moves from a Christendom and modernist mindset to a post-Christendom, postmodern mindset, its theologizing needs to change.

It is a pleasing development for the largest part of the church to have resources, such as the chapters in this book, to stimulate change. This change will bring about an invention of contextually relevant theological education for each context. Thus we will enter an era when seminaries will vary considerably from each other, still drawing on the history and the globalized conversations of the church, but specializing in the unique elements needed for greater effectiveness in mission.

It is an exciting development for the world of theological education that resources are becoming available for creating something new. It promises far greater competence in those who engage in theological education, as they are equipped for the unique context of their service.

Within the ICETE community there is a growing expectation that accreditation processes will include the elements of context-based research. That in itself will provide even greater impetus for change. Surely this will strengthen the capacity of seminaries, which will strengthen the capacity of their graduates, which will strengthen the capacity of their churches, which will flow through to their missional activity and the blessing they bring to their societies. This will lead to greater praise of the Living God, from whom all people derive their being, and to whom all people must give account.

Bibliography

Acemoglu, Daron. *Lectures in Labor Economics.* Chapter 1, "The Basic Theory of Human Capital." Accessed 30 October 2015. http://econ.lse.ac.uk/staff/spischke/ec533/Acemoglu%20Autor%20chapter%201.pdf.

ACTEA. "Standards and Procedures for Accreditation at Post-Secondary Level." 1992.

Aleshire, Daniel O. "Fifty Years of Accrediting Theological Schools," *Theological Education* 49, no. 1 (2014): 63–80.

Aristotle. *Nicomachean Ethics,* in Jowett, B. *The Works of Plato & Aristotle – 35 Works,* C&C Web Press, 2009. Book 1. Ebook.

Banks, Robert. *Reenvisioning Theological Education.* Grand Rapids, MI: Eerdmans, 1999.

Bartholomew, C., and M. Goheen. *The Drama of Scripture: Finding Our Place in the Biblical Story.* 2nd edition. Grand Rapids: Baker, 2014.

Beltrán, W. (s.f.). "La expansión pentecostal en Colombia." In Beltrán et al., *El pentecostalismo en Colombia,* 74–93.

Beltrán, W. M., I. N. Cuervo, J. D. López, J. Ravagli, G. M. Reyes, S. Rivers and C. Tejeiro. *El pentecostalismo en Colombia: Prácticas religiosas, liderazgo y participación política.* Bogotá: Centro de Estudios Sociales, 2010.

Borda Carulla, S. "Resocialization of 'Desplazados' in Small Pentecostal Congregations in Bogotá, Colombia." *Refugee Survey Quarterly* 26, no. 2 (2007): 36–46.

Cronshaw, Darren. "Reenvisioning Theological Education and Missional Spirituality." *Journal of Adult Theological Education* 9, no. 1 (2012): 9–27.

Dayton, Donald W. *Theological Roots of Pentecostalism.* Peabody, MA: Hendrickson, 2000.

Demera, J. D. "Ciudad, migración y religión: Etnografía de los recursos identitarios y de la religiosidad de los desplazados en altos de Cazucá." *Theologica Xaveriana* (2007): 303–320.

Edgar, Brian. "The Theology of Theological Education." *Evangelical Review of Theology* 29, no. 3 (2005): 208–217.

Franke, John. *The Character of Theology: An Introduction to Its Nature, Task, and Purpose.* Grand Rapids, MI: Baker Academic, 2005.

Gonzales, G., and R. Wagenaar. *Tuning Educational Structures in Europe – Final Report, Phase One,* 2003. http://www.relint.deusto.es/TUNINGProject/doc_tuning_phase1.asp. Accessed 5 May 2009.

Gudykunst, W. B. "Individualistic and Collectivistic Perspectives on Communication: An Introduction." *International Journal of Intercultural Relations* 22, no. 2 (1998): 107–134.

"Higher Education: The University Experiment." *Nature: International Weekly Journal of Science* 514 (15 October 2014). Accessed 10 November 2015. http://www.nature.com/news/higher-education-the-university-experiment-1.16133.

ICETE. "ICETE Manifesto on the Renewal of Evangelical Theological Education." http://www.icete-edu.org/manifesto/.

Jaeger, Werner. *Early Christianity and Greek Paideia*. Cambridge, MA: Harvard University Press, 1961.

Kelsey, David H. *Between Athens and Berlin: The Theological Debate*. Grand Rapids, MI: Eerdmans, 1993.

———. *To Understand God Truly: What's Theological about a Theological School*. Louisville, KY: Westminster/John Knox, 1992.

Lausanne Movement. "The Cape Town Commitment." 2011. https://www.lausanne.org/content/ctc/ctcommitment.

Lawson, Lewis A., and Victor A. Kramer, eds. *Conversations with Walker Percy*. Jackson, MS: University Press of Mississippi, 1985.

Lindhardt, M. "La Globalización Pentecostal: Difusión, Apropiación y Orientación Global." *Cultura & Religión* (2011): 117–136.

López, D. *Pentecostalismo y Misión integral*. Lima: Ediciones Puma, 2008.

———. *Pentecostalismo y Transformación social*. Buenos Aires: Ediciones Kairós, 2000.

Mafla, N. "Función de la religión en la vida de las víctimas del desplazamiento forzado en Colombia." PhD diss., Universidad Complutense de Madrid, 2012.

Migliore, Daniel. *Faith Seeking Understanding: An Introduction to Christian Theology*. Grand Rapids, MI: Eerdmans, 2004.

Mulder, M., T. Weigel, and K. Collins. "The Concept of Competence in the Development of Vocational Education and Training in Selected EU Member States: A Critical Analysis." *Journal of Vocational Education and Training* 59, no. 1 (2007): 67–88.

Murray, Stuart. *Church after Christendom*. Bletchley: Paternoster, 2005.

Peterson, Eugene. *Under the Unpredictable Plant: An Exploration in Vocational Holiness*. Grand Rapids, MI: Eerdmans, 1994.

Schleiermacher, Friedrich, and Terrence Tice. *Brief Outline of Theology as a Field of Study: Revised Translation of the 1811 and 1830 Editions*. 3rd edition. Louisville, KY: Westminster John Knox, 2011.

Tarnas, Richard. *The Passion of the Western Mind: Understanding the Ideas That Have Shaped Our World View*. New York: Harmony, 1993.

Teichler, U., and B. Kehm. "Towards a New Understanding of the Relationships between Higher Education and Employment." *European Journal of Education* 30, no. 2, (1995): 115–132. JSTOR.

Trombino, Mario. *La Filosofia Greca Arcaica e Classica*. Bologna: Poseidonia, 1997.

Tuning Management Committee. *Tuning Educational Structures in Europe*, 2006. http://tuning.unideusto.org/tuningeu/images/stories/template/General_Brochure_final_version.pdf. Accessed 20 April 2007.

Villafañe, E. *El Espíritu liberador: Hacia una ética social pentecostal latinoamericana*. Buenos Aires: Nueva Creacion; Grand Rapids, MI: Eerdmans, 1996.

Wolterstorff, N. *Educating for Shalom: Essays on Christian Higher Education*. Cambridge: Eerdmans, 2004. Kindle.

Resources

The following books are recommended to help seminaries to take the next step of researching the outcomes and impact of their graduates.

Rupen Das was the lead researcher at Arab Baptist Theological Seminary when they began the first project indicated in this book. His work *Connecting Curriculum with Context* has a very helpful section providing sample questionnaires for seminaries to adapt to their situation.

Perry Shaw was the educationalist on the faculty of Arab Baptist Theological Seminary at the time they reconceived their curriculum. The book *Transforming Theological Education* provides a rich treasure of thoughtful suggestions on curriculum redesign. His goal is to help create a more holistic educational method, content and outcome.

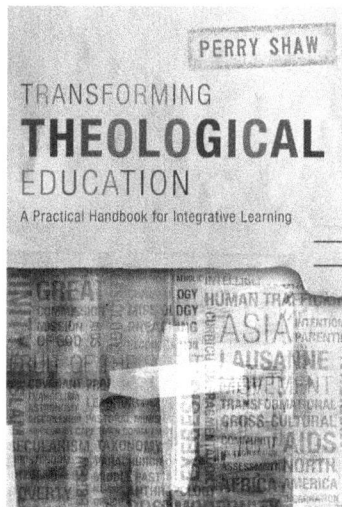

List of Contributors

Stuart Brooking, PhD, is Executive Director of Overseas Council Australia which works to fund and encourage theological institutions in the Majority World. He is part-time head of the Department of Ministry and Practice at the Australian College of Theology.

Jhohan Centeno is a professor at the Biblical Seminary of Colombia (FUSBC) in Medellín and also oversees the virtual programs. He is an authorized minister in the Foursquare Church. He has a master's degree in E-learning and is currently pursuing his doctoral studies in Theology.

Ashish Chrispal, PhD, lives in Bangalore, India. He has served the Lord Jesus Christ as a pastor, theological teacher and principal, and facilitator for theological education through Overseas Council.

Scott Cunningham, PhD. Scott's experience as a theological educator began as a missionary faculty member in Nigerian seminaries. He later served the Association for Christian Theological Education in Africa (ACTEA), assisting seminaries with accreditation. Scott currently serves the international team of Overseas Council as Executive Director.

Rupen Das, PhD, is Research Professor at Tyndale University College and Seminary in Toronto and National Director of the Canadian Bible Society. He was worked and taught in various international contexts including Amsterdam and Lebanon.

Havilah Dharamraj, PhD (Durham, UK), is the Academic Dean at the South Asia Institute of Advanced Christian Studies, where she teaches Old Testament. She is one of the editors of, and a contributor to, the *South Asia Bible Commentary*.

Elie Haddad is President of Arab Baptist Theological Seminary in Lebanon. He has a background in management and ministry. He is currently doing doctoral studies in missional ecclesiology.

Robert Heaton, PhD, is registrar at the Theological College of Zimbabwe, following decades of ministry at that institution including ten years as acting principal. He has held other leadership positions with national Christian bodies such as the Baptist Union.

Melody Mazuk has served as a theological librarian for many years in a variety of Christian colleges and seminaries worldwide. She describes herself both as a global Christian and a global theological librarian.

Ray Motsi, PhD, is President of the Theological College of Zimbabwe. His doctoral work was in Peace Building and Conflict Transformation and has worked in this area in different contexts.

Marvin Oxenham, PhD, is General Secretary of the European Evangelical Accrediting Association (EEAA) and has worked with Overseas Council. He is currently Program Leader in Theological Education at the London School of Theology.

A. N. Lal Senanayake, PhD, is Principal of Lanka Bible College and Seminary in Sri Lanka. Before joining LBCS full-time in 1993, he served as a pastor for over fifteen years. Lal also serves on the editorial board of *InSight Journal for Global Theological Education*.

Elizabeth Sendek is President of the Biblical Seminary of Colombia (Fundación Universitaria Seminario Bíblico de Colombia). She is an associate of Global Associates for Transformational Education (GATE).

Perry Shaw, EdD, is Professor of Education at Arab Baptist Theological Seminary in Beirut, Lebanon, and the author of *Transforming Theological Education*. Perry and his family have been serving in the Middle East since 1990.

Christopher Wright, PhD (Cambridge, UK), is the International Ministries Director of Langham Partnership and the author of numerous books on mission and on the Old Testament. Previously he taught at Union Biblical Seminary in Pune, India, and at All Nations Christian College in Ware, England.

Global Hub for Evangelical Theological Education

Mission

ICETE advances quality and collaboration in global theological education to strengthen and accompany the church in its mission.

Objectives

As a global hub for evangelical theological education, ICETE is recognized for its reliable capacity to:

1. Develop, disseminate, mutually validate, harmonize, and inspire quality in theological education, aimed at fostering reciprocal trust among stakeholders, including the church;

2. Cultivate worldwide relationships, stimulated through gatherings, communications for reflection, interactive dialogue, collaboration, and practice in support of the church's mission; and

3. Train, consult, and provide resources for those involved in theological education, marked by relevance, accessibility, and collaborative effectiveness.

ICETE's mission emphasizes its dual focus on quality *and* collaboration through its constituency to strengthen and accompany the church in its mission. The quality aspect of our work addresses the church-academy gap by requiring theological institutions to build strategic partnerships with churches and ministry organizations. ICETE quality assurance seeks to be an agent for change in theological institutions, and consequently in the lives of the next generation of global leaders.

Through collaborative opportunities, our impact begins with theological educators and extends exponentially to training programs, students, church leaders, and the broader community for the sake of the church. Our work targets theological educators across all sectors who prepare thousands of learners serving in hundreds of ministries.

www.icete.info

Langham
PARTNERSHIP

Langham Literature and its imprints are a ministry of Langham Partnership.

Langham Partnership is a global fellowship working in pursuit of the vision God entrusted to its founder John Stott –

to facilitate the growth of the church in maturity and Christ-likeness through raising the standards of biblical preaching and teaching.

Our vision is to see churches in the majority world equipped for mission and growing to maturity in Christ through the ministry of pastors and leaders who believe, teach and live by the Word of God.

Our mission is to strengthen the ministry of the Word of God through:
- nurturing national movements for biblical preaching
- fostering the creation and distribution of evangelical literature
- enhancing evangelical theological education

especially in countries where churches are under-resourced.

Our ministry

Langham Preaching partners with national leaders to nurture indigenous biblical preaching movements for pastors and lay preachers all around the world. With the support of a team of trainers from many countries, a multi-level programme of seminars provides practical training, and is followed by a programme for training local facilitators. Local preachers' groups and national and regional networks ensure continuity and ongoing development, seeking to build vigorous movements committed to Bible exposition.

Langham Literature provides majority world preachers, scholars and seminary libraries with evangelical books and electronic resources through publishing and distribution, grants and discounts. The programme also fosters the creation of indigenous evangelical books in many languages, through writer's grants, strengthening local evangelical publishing houses, and investment in major regional literature projects, such as one volume Bible commentaries like *The Africa Bible Commentary* and *The South Asia Bible Commentary*.

Langham Scholars provides financial support for evangelical doctoral students from the majority world so that, when they return home, they may train pastors and other Christian leaders with sound, biblical and theological teaching. This programme equips those who equip others. Langham Scholars also works in partnership with majority world seminaries in strengthening evangelical theological education. A growing number of Langham Scholars study in high quality doctoral programmes in the majority world itself. As well as teaching the next generation of pastors, graduated Langham Scholars exercise significant influence through their writing and leadership.

To learn more about Langham Partnership and the work we do visit **langham.org**

* 9 7 8 1 7 8 3 6 8 3 3 3 8 *